CIMA

E
X
A
M

P
R
A
C
T
I
C
E

K
I
T

OPERATIONAL LEVEL

PAPER F1

FINANCIAL REPORTING AND TAXATION

FOR EXAMS IN 2015/16

BPP
LEARNING MEDIA

Second edition June 2015

ISBN 9781 4727 3424 2
e-ISBN 9781 4727 3664 2

British Library Cataloguing-in-Publication Data
A catalogue record for this book
is available from the British Library

Published by

BPP Learning Media Ltd
BPP House, Aldine Place, 142/144 Uxbridge Road
London W12 8AA

www.bpp.com/learningmedia

Printed in the United Kingdom by Ricoh UK Limited

Unit 2
Wells Place
Merstham
RH1 3LG

Your learning materials, published by BPP Learning
Media Ltd, are printed on paper obtained from
traceable, sustainable sources.

Contents

Question and Answer index

Using your BPP OTQ Kit

One of the key criteria for achieving exam success is question practice. There is generally a direct correlation between candidates who study all topics and practise exam questions and those who are successful in their real exams. This Kit gives you ample opportunity for such practice throughout your preparations for your OT exam.

All questions in your exam are compulsory and all the component learning outcomes will be examined so you must **study the whole syllabus**. Selective studying will limit the number of questions you can answer and hence reduce your chances of passing. It is better to go into the exam knowing a reasonable amount about most of the syllabus rather than concentrating on a few topics to the exclusion of the rest.

Practising as many exam-style questions as possible will be the key to passing this exam. You must do questions under **timed conditions**.

Breadth of question coverage

Questions will cover the whole of the syllabus so you must study all the topics in the syllabus.

The weightings in the table below indicate the approximate proportion of study time you should spend on each topic, and is related to the number of questions per syllabus area in the exam.

F1 Financial Reporting and Taxation Syllabus topics	Weighting
A Regulatory environment for financial reporting and corporate governance	10%
B Financial accounting and reporting	45%
C Management of working capital, cash and sources of short-term finance	20%
D Fundamentals of business taxation	25%

The Objective Test exam

The Objective Test exam is a computer based assessment, which is available on demand at assessment centres all year round.

Objective Test exams in each level can be taken in any order, but candidates must pass all the OT exams for a level before they can sit the Integrated Case Study Exam for that level.

Each exam lasts for 90 minutes and the pass mark is 70%.

Results are available shortly after the test has been completed, and the results will include feedback.

The exam will be made up of different types of questions, including:

Question Type	Explanation
Multiple choice	Standard multiple choice items provide four options. 1 option is correct and the other 3 are incorrect. Incorrect options will be plausible, so you should expect to have to use detailed, syllabus-specific knowledge to identify the correct answer rather than relying on common sense.
Multiple response	A multiple response item is the same as a multiple choice question, except more than one response is required. You will normally (but not always) be told how many options you need to select.
Drag and drop	Drag and drop questions require you to drag a "token" onto a pre-defined area. These tokens can be images or text. This type of question is effective at testing the order of events, labelling a diagram or linking events to outcomes.
Gap fill	Gap fill (or "fill in the blank") questions require you to type a short numerical response. You should carefully follow the instructions in the question in terms of how to type your answer – e.g. the correct number of decimal places.
Hot spot	These questions require you to identify an area or location on an image by clicking on it. This is commonly used to identify a specific point on a graph or diagram
Drop-down list	Drop-down lists follow the same principle as multiple choice questions, in that you need to select one option from a pre-defined list. This can be used in conjunction with a gap-fill question: for example, you may be asked to key a numerical answer into a gap-fill box and then select an explanation for the approach you've taken from a drop-down list.

BPP
LEARNING MEDIA

Learning Objectives

The table below has been prepared by CIMA to help you understand the abilities that CIMA is seeking to assess.

Learning objective	Verbs used	Definition	Example question types
1 Knowledge			
What you are expected to know	• List	• Make a list of	MCQ
	• State	• Express, fully or clearly, the details of/facts of	MCQ
	• Define	• Give the exact meaning of	MCQ
2 Comprehension			
What you are expected to understand	• Describe	• Communicate the key features of	Multiple Response
	• Distinguish	• Highlight the differences between	Multiple Response
	• Explain	• Make clear or intelligible/state the meaning or purpose of	Drop down list
	• Identify	• Recognise, establish or select after consideration	Hotspot
	• Illustrate	• Use an example to describe or explain something	Drop down list
3 Application			
How you are expected to apply your knowledge	• Apply	• Put to practical use	Multiple response
	• Calculate/ compute	• Ascertain or reckon mathematically	Number entry
	• Demonstrate	• Prove the certainty or exhibit by practical means	Hotspot
	• Prepare	• Make or get ready for use	Drag and drop
	• Reconcile	• Make or prove consistent/ compatible	Drop down list
	• Solve	• Find an answer to	Number entry
	• Tabulate	• Arrange in a table	Drag and drop

Learning objective	Verbs used	Definition	Example question types
4 Analysis			
How you are expected to analyse the detail of what you have learned	• Analyse	• Examine in detail the structure of	Multiple response
	• Categorise	• Place into a defined class or division	Drag and drop
	• Compare & contrast	• Show the similarities and/or differences between	Hotspot
	• Construct	• Build up or complete	Drag and drop
	• Discuss	• Examine in detail by argument	Multiple response
	• Interpret	• Translate into intelligible or familiar terms	Multiple response
	• Prioritise	• Place in order of priority or sequence for action	Drop down list
	• Produce	• Create or bring into existence	Drag and drop
5 Evaluation			
How you are expected to use your learning to evaluate, make decisions or recommendations	• Advise	• Counsel, inform or notify	Multiple response
	• Evaluate	• Appraise or assess the value of	Multiple response
	• Recommend	• Propose a course of action	Multiple response

In your CBA, questions will be set which test up to the cognitive level of the verb in the component learning outcome in each paper's syllabus, so this means they will test up to level 5 verbs where the learning outcome permits this.

CIMA will limit the number of lower level questions in the exam – so that students will not be able to achieve the pass mark solely based on correctly answering knowledge and comprehension questions. Higher level questions, requiring candidates to demonstrate application, analysis and evaluation skills must be answered correctly for the pass mark to be reached.

Passing the F1 Objective Test exam

Tackling OTQs

- Read, and **re-read the question** to ensure you fully understand what is being asked.

- When starting to read a question, especially one with a lengthy scenario, **read the requirement first**. You will then find yourself considering the requirement as you read the data in the scenario, helping you to focus on exactly what you have to do.

- **Do not spend too much time on one question** - remember you should spend 1½ minutes, on average, per question

- If you cannot decide between two answers – look carefully and decide whether for one of the options you are making an unnecessary assumption – **do not be afraid of trusting your gut instinct**

- **Do not keep changing your mind** – research has shown that the 1st answer that appeals to you is often the correct one

- Remember that marks are awarded for correct answers, and marks will not be deducted for incorrect answers. Therefore **answer every single question**, even ones you are unsure of.

- Always submit an answer for a given question even if you do not know the answer - **never leave any answers blank**

- **Pace yourself** - you will need to work through the exam at the right speed. Too fast and your accuracy may suffer, too slow and you may run out of time. Use this Kit to practice your time keeping and approach to answering each question.

- If you are unsure about anything, remember to **ask the test administrator** before the test begins. Once the clock begins ticking, interruptions will not be allowed

- Remember to **keep moving on!** You may be presented with a question which you simply cannot answer due to difficulty or if the wording is too vague. If you have only approximately 90 seconds per question, and you find yourself spending five minutes determining the answer for a question then your time management skills are poor and you are wasting valuable time.

- If you finish the exam with time to spare, use the rest of the time to **review your answers** and to make sure that you answered every OTQ

Demonstrating your understanding of F1

The F1 examiner will expect you to demonstrate the following:

Origins and authority of regulations	You must be able to **explain** how regulations are developed and **discuss** why they are necessary. Knowledge of the CIMA *Code of Ethics* should underpin all your studies and conduct at work.
The principal financial statements	You must be able to **explain** the main elements and **produce** the key financial statements in accordance with relevant IASs/IFRSs and ethical considerations.
Sources of short-term finance and working capital	You must be able to **describe** sources of short-term finance, **evaluate** the working capital position and **analyse** the short-term cash position.
Taxation	You must be able to **discuss** types of taxation and **explain** taxation in relation to international operations. You will also be required to **produce** tax computations.

All OTQs in all the exams are worth the same number of marks, both in this Kit and in the real exam. However this is an approximate guide: some OTQs are very short and just require a factual selection, which you either know or you don't, while others are more complex, which will inevitably take more time. Note that the real exam will be balanced such that the 'difficulty' of the exam will be fair for all students – the OTQs in this Kit have also been balanced in a similar way.

Using the solutions and feedback

Avoid looking at the answer until you have finished a question. It can be very tempting to do so, but unless you give the question a proper attempt under exam conditions you will not know how you would have coped with it in the real exam scenario.

When you do look at the answer, compare it with your own and give some thought to why your answer was different, if it was.

If you did not reach the correct answer make sure that you work through the explanation or workings provided, to see where you went wrong. If you think that you do not understand the principle involved, work through and revise the point again, to ensure that you will understand it if it occurs in the exam.

Objective test questions

1 Regulation and corporate governance

1.1 **Which one of the following bodies is responsible for reviewing new financial reporting issues and issuing guidance on the application of IFRSs?**

☐ The International Accounting Standards Board
☐ The IFRS Foundation
☐ The IFRS Interpretations Committee
☐ The IFRS Advisory Council

1.2 **Which one of the following is responsible for governance and fundraising in relation to the development of International Financial Reporting Standards?**

☐ International Accounting Standards Board
☐ IFRS Interpretations Committee
☐ IFRS Foundation Trustees
☐ IFRS Advisory Council

1.3 **Which of the following provides advice to the International Accounting Standards Board (IASB) as well as informing the IASB of the implications of proposed standards for users and preparers of financial statements?**

☐ The IFRS Advisory Council
☐ The IFRS Interpretations Committee
☐ The IFRS Foundation
☐ The Trustees

1.4 **Corporate governance can be best defined as:**

☐ The system by which companies are directed and controlled
☐ A system of control designed to manage risk
☐ A system that allows for corrective action and penalising mismanagement
☐ The system that ensures director accountability to shareholders and stakeholders
☐ The board being able to take decisions that enhance the prosperity of the company

1.5 **Which of the following would NOT be regarded as good practice for the nomination committee?**

☐ The nomination committee should consider the need to attract board members from a diversity of backgrounds

☐ The nomination committee should consist entirely of executive directors

☐ The nomination committee should regularly review the structure, size and composition of the board

☐ The nomination committee should consider whether non-executive directors are spending enough time on their duties

☐ The nomination committee should use an external search consultancy and open advertising when recruiting a chairman

1.6 The setting of International Financial Reporting Standards is carried out by co-operation between the IFRS Foundation, the IFRS Advisory Council and the IFRS Interpretations Committee.

Which of the following reports to the International Accounting Standards Board (IASB)?

☐ The IFRS Foundation
☐ The IFRS Advisory Committee
☐ The IFRS Interpretations Committee
☐ The IFRS Advisory Committee and the IFRS Interpretations Committee

1.7 **Which THREE of the following are the responsibilities of the IFRS Foundation Trustees?**

☐ Issuing International Financial Reporting Standards

☐ Approving the annual budget of the IASB

☐ Enforcing International Financial Reporting Standards

☐ Reviewing the strategy of the IASB and its effectiveness

☐ Appointing the members of the IASB, the IFRS Interpretations Committee and the IFRS Advisory Council

1.8 **Which of the following statements is/ are true?**

☐ The IFRS Interpretations Committee is a forum for the IASB to consult with the outside world

☐ The IFRS Foundation produces IFRSs. The IFRS Foundation is overseen by the IASB

☐ One of the objectives of the IFRS Foundation is to bring about convergence of national accounting standards and IFRSs

1.9 **Which FOUR of the following are characteristics of a purely principles-based approach to corporate governance?**

☐ It focuses on objectives
☐ It can be applied across different legal jurisdictions
☐ It can stress those areas where rules cannot easily be applied
☐ It puts the emphasis on investors making up their own minds
☐ It includes definite targets for companies to meet

1.10 **Which TWO of the following are characteristics of a rules-based approach to corporate governance?**

☐ It allows companies to operate on a comply or explain basis
☐ It emphasises measurable achievements by companies
☐ It covers all eventualities
☐ It can easily be applied in jurisdictions where the letter of the law is stressed
☐ It can easily be applied across different legal jurisdictions

2 External audit

2.1   Which of the following statements properly reflects the objective of an audit?

The objective of an audit is to enable the auditors to:

- ☐   Form an opinion as to the truth and fairness of a set of financial statements
- ☐   Detect all frauds in the operation of a business and to report them to shareholders
- ☐   Provide a guarantee that the company will continue as a going concern
- ☐   Provide a certificate to the directors that the financial statements are 100% accurate

2.2   Which of the following is NOT a necessary component of the audit report for a limited liability company?

- ☐   The identity of the auditor

- ☐   A statement specifying that the auditor has complied with International Standards on Auditing

- ☐   Identification of the accounting convention adopted by management in preparing the financial statements

- ☐   Identification of the financial statements audited

2.3   The financial statements of X Co include a receivables balance which is material in amount. The auditors do not believe that any part of the balance will be paid. This problem is not considered to be fundamental to a user's understanding of the financial statements.

What form of audit opinion should be given?

- ☐   Unmodified opinion
- ☐   Modified - adverse opinion
- ☐   Modified - qualified opinion (due to material misstatement)
- ☐   Modified - qualified opinion (due to insufficient appropriate audit evidence)

2.4   An auditor gives an audit report that contains an 'adverse opinion'.

What does this mean?

- ☐   The auditor obtains sufficient appropriate evidence, but concludes that misstatements are both material and pervasive to the financial statements

- ☐   The auditor cannot obtain sufficient appropriate audit evidence in order to enable him to give an opinion on the financial statements

- ☐   The auditor concludes that the financial statements are free from material misstatement

- ☐   The auditor obtains sufficient appropriate evidence, and concludes that misstatements are material, but not pervasive to the financial statements

2.5   Which of the following terms represents the form of modification to an audit opinion arising from the situation where the auditor has not be able to obtain sufficient appropriate audit evidence and the auditor considers this to be pervasive?

- ☐   Disclaimer of opinion
- ☐   Qualified opinion
- ☐   Emphasis of matter paragraph
- ☐   Adverse opinion

2.6 Daffy makes and sells medical equipment and has a sizeable research and development unit. The directors have identified three material applied research projects whose results they hope will be developed into viable products. They have therefore capitalised the expenditure on these projects and will amortise it over three years. The directors believe this treatment is acceptable and refuse to change it. The accounts fully disclose the treatment adopted. The treatment of the research projects is not fundamental to user's understanding of the accounts.

What form should the audit opinion take?

☐ Modified - qualified opinion due to material misstatement
☐ Modified - adverse opinion due to pervasive material misstatement
☐ Unmodified, but including an emphasis of matter paragraph about the research projects
☐ Unmodified

2.7 Which **FOUR** of the following are explicit elements of an unmodified external audit report according to ISA 700 *Forming an opinion and reporting on financial statements*?

☐ A statement of management's and auditor's responsibilities
☐ A statement of the auditor's opinion as to the truth and fairness of the financial statements
☐ A statement that the audit was conducted in accordance with International Standards on Auditing
☐ A statement that the audit includes evaluating the appropriateness of the accounting policies used
☐ A statement as to the going concern status of the company

2.8 The directors of an entity are refusing to amend the financial statements to take account of a customer who went bankrupt after the year-end and who owed the entity $10,000 at the year-end. This amount is material.

What type of audit opinion should be issued as a result?

☐ Qualified opinion
☐ Adverse opinion
☐ Unmodified opinion with emphasis of matter paragraph
☐ Disclaimer of opinion

2.9 Which of the following matters are normally covered by the auditor's report?

☐ Whether the company has kept proper accounting records

☐ Whether the financial statements are in agreement with the accounting records

☐ Whether the financial statements have been prepared in accordance with the relevant legislation and accounting standards

☐ Whether other information presented with the financial statements is consistent with them

2.10 Which of the following are **NOT** one of those matters?

☐ The financial statements have been prepared by a qualified accountant

☐ Proper accounting records have been kept

☐ The financial statements have been prepared in accordance with local legislation and relevant accounting standards

☐ The financial statements are in agreement with accounting records

3 Ethics

3.1 **Which of these would constitute an advocacy threat?**

☐   The audit firm being sued by the client
☐   The audit firm and the client being sued by a third party
☐   The audit firm suing the client for non-payment of fees
☐   The audit firm giving evidence in court on behalf of the client

3.2 The CIMA Code of Ethics identifies five types of threat to the fundamental principles.

Which of the following is NOT one of these types of threat?

☐   Fraud
☐   Self-interest
☐   Self-review
☐   Advocacy
☐   Familiarity

3.3 Safeguards can be put in place to avoid threats to independence arising from a specific engagement.

Which of these is NOT a safeguard?

☐   Rotating senior assurance team personnel
☐   Discussing ethical issues with those charged with governance of the client
☐   Getting another firm to perform part of the engagement
☐   Recruiting senior management for the client

3.4 A professional accountant in business may be involved in a wide variety of work.

Which of these functions will he NOT be carrying out?

☐   Preparing financial statements
☐   Auditing financial statements
☐   Preparing budgets and forecasts
☐   Preparing the management letter provided to the auditors

3.5 Three of the following are recognised advantages of a principles based approach to ethical codes.

Which ONE is the exception?

☐   Encourages proactive discussion of issues
☐   Encourages consistent application of rules
☐   Suits complex situations and evolving environments
☐   Encourages professional development

3.6 A professional accountant is required under the CIMA Code of Ethics to comply with five fundamental principles.

These include:

☐   Integrity, Objectivity, Reliability
☐   Professional competence and due care, Confidentiality, Integrity
☐   Morality, Objectivity, Professional behaviour
☐   Efficiency, Confidentiality, Professional competence and due care

3.7 A qualified accountant holds a number of shares in his employing company, and has become eligible for a profit-related bonus for the first time.

What type of threat could this represent to his objectivity when preparing the company's financial statements?

- ☐ Self-interest
- ☐ Self-review
- ☐ Intimidation
- ☐ Familiarity

3.8 While at a party at the weekend, you meet a client of yours who is clearly very concerned about some VAT issues. You know enough about VAT to carry out your daily work, but you are not an expert on the areas of imports and exports on which your client is asking your opinion.

What ethical issue does this situation raise?

- ☐ Objectivity
- ☐ Professional competence and due care
- ☐ Professional behaviour
- ☐ Confidentiality

3.9 **Which of the following is an advantage of a principles-based ethical code?**

- ☐ It can easily be legally enforced
- ☐ It provides rules to be followed in all circumstances
- ☐ It encourages compliance by requiring a professional person to actively consider the issues
- ☐ It can be narrowly interpreted, making it easy for the professional to see whether or not the Code has been violated

3.10 **Which of the following is NOT a circumstance where disclosure of confidential information is permitted under the CIMA Code of Ethics?**

- ☐ Disclosure of information when authorised by the client
- ☐ Disclosure of information to advance the interests of a new client
- ☐ Disclosure of information to protect the professional interests of an accountant in a legal action
- ☐ Disclosure of information when required by law

4 The Conceptual Framework

4.1 **Which of the following is NOT true regarding the IASB's *Conceptual framework for financial reporting*?**

- ☐ It encourages companies to present information faithfully
- ☐ It gives a framework to be followed in all circumstances when preparing and presenting a set of financial statements
- ☐ It is an accounting standard that companies have to comply with
- ☐ It replaced the original framework in 2010

4.2 Which of the following is NOT an element of the financial statements as covered in the IASB's *Conceptual Framework for Financial Reporting*?

☐ Assets
☐ Liabilities
☐ Profits
☐ Equity

4.3 Which two of the following statements describe comparability?

☐ The non-cash effects of transactions should be reflected in the financial statements for the accounting period in which they occur and not in the period where any cash involved is received or paid

☐ Similar items should be treated in the same way from one period to the next

☐ Information must have a predictive and/ or confirmatory value

☐ Similar items within a single set of financial statements should be given similar accounting treatment

4.4 Which of the following options correctly describes the status of the IASB's *Conceptual framework for financial reporting*?

☐ It carries the force of law
☐ Compliance ensures that a true and fair view is given
☐ No departures are allowed from the contents of the framework
☐ It provides a framework for the formulation of accounting standards

4.5 Which THREE of the following options are advantages of the IASB's *Conceptual framework for financial reporting*?

☐ A coherent conceptual framework can suggest solutions to many issues
☐ It helps to reduce the scope for individual judgement and potential subjectivity
☐ It demands that financial statements contain relevant information
☐ It is consistent with US GAAP

4.6 Which three of the following are included in the purpose of the IASB's *Conceptual framework for financial reporting*?

☐ It assists national standard setting bodies in developing national standards

☐ To assist auditors in forming an opinion as to whether financial statements conform with IASs/IFRSs

☐ It assists the Board of the IASB in the development of future International Financial Reporting Standards and in its review of existing standards

☐ A conceptual framework eliminates misleading financial statements as there are always fundamental principles to refer to

4.7 Which TWO of the following are the fundamental qualitative characteristics of financial information per the IASB's *Conceptual framework for financial reporting*?

☐ Consistency
☐ Understandability
☐ Comparability
☐ Reliability
☐ Relevance
☐ Faithful representation
☐ Predictive value

4.8 Fair value is defined in IFRS 13.

Which of the following options best describes fair value?

☐   The value which a company places on its assets and liabilities

☐   The market price at which an asset or liability should be offered for sale

☐   The price that would be received to sell an asset or paid to transfer a liability in an orderly transaction between market participants at the measurement date

☐   The carrying values of a company's assets and liabilities

4.9 **Which two of the following are NOT elements of financial statements per the IASB's *Conceptual Framework for Financial Reporting*?**

☐   Profits
☐   Assets
☐   Income
☐   Equity
☐   Losses
☐   Expenses

4.10 **According to the IASB's *Conceptual framework for financial reporting*, the statement of profit or loss and other comprehensive income shows an entity's:**

☐   Economic resources
☐   Financial performance
☐   Changes in resources and claims
☐   Financial adaptability

5 Presentation of published financial statements

5.1 **In accordance with IAS 1 *Presentation of financial statements*, which of the following MUST be disclosed on the face of the statement of profit or loss rather than by way of a note?**

☐   Other operating income
☐   Depreciation
☐   Finance costs
☐   Dividends paid

5.2 **Which of the following is true concerning the statement of changes in equity?**

☐   It reports all realised profits and losses only
☐   It does not include revaluation surpluses
☐   It includes other comprehensive income
☐   All of the above

5.3 BCW Co's statement of financial position showed capital and reserves figures for the years ended 31/12/X1 and 31/12/X2, as indicated in the table. All figures are in $'000s.

	20X2	20X1
Ordinary share capital	500	400
Share premium	20	0
Revaluation surplus	150	75
Retained earnings	400	340
	1,070	815

Dividends of $50,000 were paid during the year ended 31.12.X2.

What is BCW Co's total comprehensive income for the year as reported in the statement of profit and loss and other comprehensive income?

☐ $185,000
☐ $135,000
☐ $255,000
☐ $110,000

5.4 IAS 8 *Accounting policies, changes in accounting estimates and errors* provides guidance as to how to account for prior period errors.

Which TWO of the following options do NOT describe a prior period error?

☐ A material decrease in the valuation of the opening inventory resulting from a change in legislation affecting the saleability of the company's products. This legislation was retrospective and was suddenly announced after the financial statements for the previous year had been agreed

☐ The discovery of a significant fraud in a foreign subsidiary resulting in a write-down in the valuation of its assets. The perpetrators have confessed to the fraud which goes back at least 5 years

☐ The company has material underprovision for income tax arising from the use of incorrect data by the tax advisors acting for the company

☐ A deterioration in sales performance has led to the directors restating their methods for the calculation of the general irrecoverable debt provision

5.5 **Which of the following is NOT a reason for considering segmental information to be useful?**

☐ Users can better assess risks and rewards
☐ The impact of disposals is highlighted
☐ Users can compare product results year on year
☐ Disaggregating the information enables more in-depth analysis

5.6 D Co's transactions and results for the period to 31 December 20X9 are shown in the table:

	$m
Profit for the period	29
Surplus on property 1 revaluation	14
Deficit on property 2 revaluation	(7)
Issue of share capital	1

Property 2 had previously been revalued upwards.

What amount would appear in the statement of changes in equity as total comprehensive income for the period?

☐ $30m
☐ $36m
☐ $37m
☐ $43m

5.7 *DFG's* trial balance at 31 March 20X7:

	Notes	$'000	$'000
5% Loan notes (issued 20X5, redeemable 20X9)			280
Administrative expenses		180	
Cash and cash equivalents			63
Cost of sales		554	
Distribution costs		140	
Equity dividend paid 1 September 20X6		55	
Income tax	(i)	10	
Inventory at 31 March 20X7		186	
Land and buildings at cost	(ii)	960	
Loan interest paid		7	
Ordinary Shares $1 each, fully paid at 1 April 20X6			560
Plant and equipment at cost	(ii)	480	
Provision for buildings depreciation at 1 April 20X6	(iv)		33
Provision for plant and equipment depreciation at 1 April 20X6	(v)		234
Retained earnings at 1 April 20X6			121
Sales revenue	(vi)		1,275
Share premium			120
Trade payables			61
Trade receivables		175	
		2,747	2,747

Additional information:

(i)   The income tax balance in the trial balance is a result of the under provision of tax for the year ended 31 March 20X6.

(ii)   There were no sales of non-current assets during the year ended 31 March 20X7.

(iii)   The tax due for the year ended 31 March 20X7 is estimated at $52,000.

(iv)   Depreciation is charged on buildings using the straight line method at 3% per annum. The cost of land included in land and buildings is $260,000. Buildings depreciation is treated as an administrative expense.

(v)   Up to 31 March 20X6 all plant and equipment was depreciated using the straight line method at 12.5%. However some plant and equipment has been wearing out and needing to be replaced on average after six years. DFG management have therefore decided that from 1 April 20X6 the expected useful life of this type of plant and equipment should be changed to a total of six years from acquisition. The plant and equipment affected was purchased on 1 April 20X2 and had an original cost of $120,000. This plant and equipment is estimated to have no residual value. All plant and equipment depreciation should be charged to cost of sales.

(vi)   The sales revenue for the year to 31 March 20X7 includes $15,000 received from a new overseas customer. The $15,000 was a 10% deposit for an order of $150,000 worth of goods. DFG is still waiting for the results of the new customer's credit reference and at 31 March 20X7 has not despatched any goods.

What are the amounts for revenue and current assets that will be included in DFG's financial statements for the year ended 31 March 20X7?

$'000

Revenue	[ ]
Current assets	[ ]

5.8   *DFG's* trial balance at 31 March 20X7.

	Notes	$'000	$'000
5% Loan notes (issued 20X5, redeemable 20X9)			280
Administrative expenses		180	
Cash and cash equivalents			63
Cost of sales		554	
Distribution costs		140	
Equity dividend paid 1 September 20X6		55	
Income tax	(i)	10	
Inventory at 31 March 20X7		186	
Land and buildings at cost	(ii)	960	
Loan interest paid		7	
Ordinary Shares $1 each, fully paid at 1 April 20X6			560
Plant and equipment at cost	(ii)	480	
Provision for buildings depreciation at 1 April 20X6	(iv)		33
Provision for plant and equipment depreciation at 1 April 20X6	(v)		234
Retained earnings at 1 April 20X6			121
Sales revenue	(vi)		1,275
Share premium			120
Trade payables			61
Trade receivables		175	
		2,747	2,747

Additional information:

(i)   The income tax balance in the trial balance is a result of the under provision of tax for the year ended 31 March 20X6.

(ii)   There were no sales of non-current assets during the year ended 31 March 20X7.

(iii) The tax due for the year ended 31 March 20X7 is estimated at $52,000.

(iv)   Depreciation is charged on buildings using the straight line method at 3% per annum. The cost of land included in land and buildings is $260,000. Buildings depreciation is treated as an administrative expense.

(v)   Up to 31 March 20X6 all plant and equipment was depreciated using the straight line method at 12.5%. However some plant and equipment has been wearing out and needing to be replaced on average after six years. DFG management have therefore decided that from 1 April 20X6 the expected useful life of this type of plant and equipment should be changed to a total of six years from acquisition. The plant and equipment affected was purchased on 1 April 20X2 and had an original cost of $120,000. This plant and equipment is estimated to have no residual value. All plant and equipment depreciation should be charged to cost of sales.

(vi)   The sales revenue for the year to 31 March 20X7 includes $15,000 received from a new overseas customer. The $15,000 was a 10% deposit for an order of $150,000 worth of goods. DFG is still waiting for the results of the new customer's credit reference and at 31 March 20X7 has not despatched any goods.

The amount for cost of sales that will be included in DFG's statement of profit or loss and other comprehensive income for the year ended 31 March 20X7 is:

$'000 [   ]

5.9   *DFG's* trial balance at 31 March 20X7:

	Notes	$'000	$'000
5% Loan notes (issued 20X5, redeemable 20X9)			280
Administrative expenses		180	
Cash and cash equivalents			63
Cost of sales		554	
Distribution costs		140	
Equity dividend paid 1 September 20X6		55	
Income tax	(i)	10	
Inventory at 31 March 20X7		186	
Land and buildings at cost	(ii)	960	
Loan interest paid		7	
Ordinary Shares $1 each, fully paid at 1 April 20X6			560
Plant and equipment at cost	(ii)	480	
Provision for buildings depreciation at 1 April 20X6	(iv)		33
Provision for plant and equipment depreciation at 1 April 20X6	(v)		234
Retained earnings at 1 April 20X6			121
Sales revenue	(vi)		1,275
Share premium			120
Trade payables			61
Trade receivables		175	
		2,747	2,747

Additional information:

(i)   The income tax balance in the trial balance is a result of the under provision of tax for the year ended 31 March 20X6.

(ii)   There were no sales of non-current assets during the year ended 31 March 20X7.

(iii)   The tax due for the year ended 31 March 20X7 is estimated at $52,000.

(iv)   Depreciation is charged on buildings using the straight line method at 3% per annum. The cost of land included in land and buildings is $260,000. Buildings depreciation is treated as an administrative expense.

(v)   Up to 31 March 20X6 all plant and equipment was depreciated using the straight line method at 12.5%. However some plant and equipment has been wearing out and needing to be replaced on average after six years. DFG management have therefore decided that from 1 April 20X6 the expected useful life of this type of plant and equipment should be changed to a total of six years from acquisition. The plant and equipment affected was purchased on 1 April 20X2 and had an original cost of $120,000. This plant and equipment is estimated to have no residual value. All plant and equipment depreciation should be charged to cost of sales.

(vi)   The sales revenue for the year to 31 March 20X7 includes $15,000 received from a new overseas customer. The $15,000 was a 10% deposit for an order of $150,000 worth of goods. DFG is still waiting for the results of the new customer's credit reference and at 31 March 20X7 has not despatched any goods.

The amounts for administrative expenses and finance charge that will be included in DFG's statement of profit or loss and other comprehensive income for the year ended 31 March 20X7 are:

$'000

Administrative expenses [   ]

Finance charge [   ]

5.10   *DFG's* trial balance at 31 March 20X7:

	Notes	$'000	$'000
5% Loan notes (issued 20X5, redeemable 20X9)			280
Administrative expenses		180	
Cash and cash equivalents			63
Cost of sales		554	
Distribution costs		140	
Equity dividend paid 1 September 20X6		55	
Income tax	(i)	10	
Inventory at 31 March 20X7		186	
Land and buildings at cost	(ii)	960	
Loan interest paid		7	
Ordinary Shares $1 each, fully paid at 1 April 20X6			560
Plant and equipment at cost	(ii)	480	
Provision for buildings depreciation at 1 April 20X6	(iv)		33
Provision for plant and equipment depreciation at 1 April 20X6	(v)		234
Retained earnings at 1 April 20X6			121
Sales revenue	(vi)		1,275
Share premium			120
Trade payables			61
Trade receivables		175	
		2,747	2,747

Additional information:

(i)   The income tax balance in the trial balance is a result of the under provision of tax for the year ended 31 March 20X6.

(ii)   There were no sales of non-current assets during the year ended 31 March 20X7.

(iii)   The tax due for the year ended 31 March 20X7 is estimated at $52,000.

(iv)   Depreciation is charged on buildings using the straight line method at 3% per annum. The cost of land included in land and buildings is $260,000. Buildings depreciation is treated as an administrative expense.

(v)   Up to 31 March 20X6 all plant and equipment was depreciated using the straight line method at 12.5%. However some plant and equipment has been wearing out and needing to be replaced on average after six years. DFG management have therefore decided that from 1 April 20X6 the expected useful life of this type of plant and equipment should be changed to a total of six years from acquisition. The plant and equipment affected was purchased on 1 April 20X2 and had an original cost of $120,000. This plant and equipment is estimated to have no residual value. All plant and equipment depreciation should be charged to cost of sales.

(vi)   The sales revenue for the year to 31 March 20X7 includes $15,000 received from a new overseas customer. The $15,000 was a 10% deposit for an order of $150,000 worth of goods. DFG is still waiting for the results of the new customer's credit reference and at 31 March 20X7 has not despatched any goods.

The amounts for the tax expense, current tax payable, share capital and share premium that will be included in DFG's financial statements for the year ended 31 March 20X7 are:

	$'000
Tax expense	
Current tax payable	
Share capital	
Share premium	

6 Non-current assets I

6.1 Which THREE of the following costs can be included in the total cost of producing an asset by a company for its own use?

- ☐ Directly attributable labour costs
- ☐ A reasonable proportion of indirect costs
- ☐ Interest on capital borrowed to finance production of the asset
- ☐ Depreciation charges for the asset
- ☐ On-going maintenance charges for the asset

6.2 Which TWO of the following can be included in the calculation of the cost of a non-current asset as per IAS 16?

- ☐ For a purchased asset, expenses incidental (directly attributable) to the acquisition of the asset
- ☐ For a manufactured asset, only the direct costs of production
- ☐ For a manufactured asset, direct costs of production plus a reasonable proportion of indirect costs
- ☐ Annual maintenance costs

6.3 BI owns a building which it uses as its offices, warehouse and garage. The land is carried as a separate non-current tangible asset in the statement of financial position.

BI has a policy of regularly revaluing its non-current tangible assets. The original cost of the building in October 20X2 was $1,000,000; it was assumed to have a remaining useful life of 20 years at that date, with no residual value. The building was revalued on 30 September 20X4 by a professional valuer at $1,800,000.

The economic climate had deteriorated during 20X5, causing BI to carry out an impairment review of its assets at 30 September 20X5. BI's building was valued at a market value of $1,500,000 on 30 September 20X5 by an independent valuer.

Calculate the impairment loss suffered at 30 September 20X5 and write in the second box whether it should be recognised as part of BI's profit or loss for the period or in other comprehensive income.

$ ☐☐☐☐☐☐☐ ☐☐☐☐☐☐☐

6.4 IAS 16 *Property, plant and equipment* requires non-current assets to be depreciated using:

- ☐ A method that allocates the cost as fairly as possible
- ☐ A method that allocates the depreciable amount as fairly as possible
- ☐ The straight line method or any similar method
- ☐ The straight line or reducing balance method

6.5 Bradley Co depreciates non-current assets at 20% per annum on a reducing balance basis. All non-current assets were purchased on 1 October 20X3. The carrying amount on 30 September 20X6 is $40,000.

What is the accumulated depreciation to the nearest thousand dollars as on that date?

$ ☐☐☐☐☐

6.6 Wilson has leased a building for 10 years and is setting up a new production plant.

Which of the following should NOT be capitalised as part of the cost of the production plant?

- ☐ Transport costs delivering machinery to the plant
- ☐ The cost of dismantling the production plant after 10 years
- ☐ Initial operating losses while the production plant reaches planned performance
- ☐ Fees paid to engineers overseeing the installation

6.7 A ship requires a safety inspection every three years as a condition of being allowed to operate. The cost of the inspection is $10,000.

How should this cost be treated in the financial statements?

- ☐ Accrued for over three years and charged to maintenance expense
- ☐ Provided for in advance and charged to maintenance expense
- ☐ Charged in full to profit or loss when the expenditure takes place
- ☐ Capitalised and depreciated over the period to the next inspection

6.8 A company purchased a machine for $50,000 on 1 January 20X1. It was judged to have a 5-year useful life with a residual value of $5,000. On 31 December 20X2 $15,000 was spent on an upgrade to the machine. This extended its remaining useful life to 5 years, with the same residual value. During 20X3, the market for the product declined and the machine was sold on 1 January 20X4 for $7,000.

What was the loss on disposal?

- ☐ $31,000
- ☐ $35,000
- ☐ $31,600
- ☐ $35,600

6.9 The components of the cost of a major item of equipment are given below.

	$
Purchase price	780,000
Import duties	117,000
Sales tax (refundable)	78,000
Site preparation costs	30,000
Installation costs	28,000
Initial operating losses before the asset reaches planned performance	50,000
Estimated cost of dismantling and removal of the asset, required to be recognised as a provision	100,000
	1,183,000

What amount may be recognised as the cost of the asset, according to IAS 16 *Property, plant and equipment*?

- ☐ $956,000
- ☐ $1,105,000
- ☐ $1,055,000
- ☐ $1,183,000

6.10 IAS 16 *Property, plant and equipment* requires an asset to be measured at cost on its original recognition in the financial statements.

EW used its own staff, assisted by contractors when required, to construct a new warehouse for its own use.

Which ONE of the following costs would NOT be included in attributable costs of the non-current asset?

- ☐ Clearance of the site prior to work commencing

- ☐ Professional surveyors' fees for managing the construction work

- ☐ EW's own staff wages for time spent working on the construction

- ☐ An allocation of EW's administration costs, based on EW staff time spent on the construction as a percentage of the total staff time

7 Non-current assets II

7.1 Which THREE of the following are required in order for a property to be defined as an investment property according to IAS 40: Investment property?

☐ An investment in land and/or buildings
☐ A freehold property
☐ Held for its investment potential
☐ Not occupied by the reporting entity for its own purposes

7.2 A company moves out of one of its buildings and rents it out. The building is revalued on being reclassified as an investment property and a revaluation surplus of $6m results.

Where will this surplus be recognised?

☐ In other comprehensive income as a revaluation gain
☐ In the statement of changes in equity as an addition to retained earnings
☐ In profit or loss as investment income
☐ In profit or loss as a gain on revaluation of an investment property

7.3 Which TWO of the following statements are true according to IAS 20 *Government grants*?

☐ IAS 20 allows capital grants to be credited to revenue over the expected life of the asset in three ways

☐ One method of accounting for capital grants is to reduce the acquisition cost of the non-current asset by the amount of the grant and charging depreciation on the reduced amount

☐ The final profit figure is different depending on the method chosen for accounting for government grants

☐ Grants relating to income are a credit to profit or loss and these may be deducted from related expenses

☐ Government grants can be recognised in the financial statements even if there is doubt as to whether the entity can comply with conditions attached to the grant

7.4 Z Co has the following loans in place during the year to 30 June 20X4:

	1 July 20X3	30 June 20X4
	$m	$m
8% bank loan (repayable 20X9)	100	100
10% bank loan (repayable 20X8)	60	60
7.5% debenture (repayable 20X6)	100	

The debenture was issued to fund the construction of a qualifying asset X, the construction of which began on 1 October 20X3.

At the beginning of the year the construction of qualifying asset Y began using the existing borrowings, funds being drawn down on I July 20X3 ($20 million) and 31 December 20X3 ($30 million).

What are the borrowing costs in $s to be capitalised for the construction of asset Y?

$ ☐

7.5 Devon Homes Co has renovated an old warehouse and converted it into six luxury apartments. To finance the project, it took out a loan of $100 million on 1 October 20X2. The loan carries no interest but is repayable on 30 September 20X5 at a premium of $33.10 million (the total amount to be repaid is $133.10 million). This equates to an effective interest rate of 10%.

Construction began on 1 October 20X2. Three of the apartments were completed on 30 September 20X4 and the remainder were completed on 30 September 20X5. Devon Homes has a policy of capitalising borrowing costs on construction projects wherever possible.

What is the total amount of borrowing costs that can be included in the cost of the conversion?

$ [   ]

7.6 On 1 January 20X1 an entity purchased a property for $4 million for its investment potential.

The land was valued at $1.5 million and the buildings at $2.5 million. The property's remaining life was 50 years.

On 31 December 20X1 the property was valued at $4.2 million (land $1.7 million and buildings $2.5 million).

The property is to be accounted for under IAS 40 *Investment property* using the fair value model.

Place the amounts given to complete the table for the year ended 31 December 20X1.

Investment property depreciation ☐
Gain on investment property ☐

- ☐ (i) $0
- ☐ (ii) $50000
- ☐ (iii) $280000
- ☐ (iv) $84000
- ☐ (v) $150000
- ☐ (vi) $200000

7.7 **Which TWO of the following statements are correct in relation to IAS 20 *Government grants*?**

- ☐ The standard requires grants to be recognised as income over the relevant periods to match them with the related costs which they have received to compensate

- ☐ Grants should be credited directly to equity

- ☐ Grants should always be a credit to income on a receipts basis

- ☐ An entity should recognise government grants as soon as it has reasonable assurance that the entity will actually receive the grant

---

7.8 An entity receives a 25% grant towards the cost of a new item of machinery, which cost $400,000. The machinery has an expected life of eight years and a nil residual value. The expected profits of the entity, before accounting for depreciation on the new machine or the grant, amount to $600,000 per annum in each year of the machinery's life.

The entity has chosen to treat the capital grant by deducting the grant to arrive at the carrying value of the asset.

Calculate the annual profit after depreciation and the carrying amount of the asset in year 3

	$
Annual Profit after depreciation	[ ]
Carrying amount of the asset in year 3	[ ]

7.9 According to IAS 23: *Borrowing Costs* which TWO of the following statements are correct?

☐ A qualifying asset is an asset that takes a substantial period of time to get ready for its intended use or sale

☐ Where specific borrowings have been used to finance the acquisition, construction or production of an asset the borrowing costs may be capitalised or expensed under finance costs in the statement of profit or loss and other comprehensive income

☐ Borrowing costs are defined as interest and other costs incurred by the entity in connection with the borrowing of funds

☐ If active development is interrupted for any extended periods the entity may still capitalise any borrowing costs during those periods

☐ Funds borrowed may be invested before they are actually used on the qualifying asset, the investment income should be recorded as finance income in the statement of profit or loss and other comprehensive income

7.10 Which ONE of the following statements is not true in accordance with IAS 23 *Borrowing costs*?

☐ Interest on bank overdrafts and short term and long term borrowings may be included in borrowing costs

☐ Financial assets and inventories that are manufactured, or otherwise produced over a short period of time are qualifying assets

☐ Where borrowing costs are obtained generally, but are applied in part to obtaining a qualifying asset, then the amount of borrowing costs eligible for capitalisation is found by applying the 'capitalisation rate'

☐ In relation to borrowing costs the following should be disclosed: the amount of borrowing costs capitalised during the period and also the capitalisation rate

8 Non-current assets III

8.1 Which THREE of the following accounting policies WOULD contravene International Financial Reporting Standards if adopted by a company?

☐ Purchased goodwill is written off immediately against reserves

☐ Land on which the company's buildings stand is not depreciated

☐ Internally generated brands are capitalised at fair value as advised by independent consultants

☐ In calculating depreciation, the estimated useful life of an asset is taken as half the actual estimated useful life as a measure of prudence

8.2 Which ONE of the following CANNOT be recognised as an intangible non-current asset in GHK's statement of financial position at 30 September 20X1?

☐ GHK spent $12,000 researching a new type of product. The research is expected to lead to a new product line in 3 years' time

☐ GHK purchased another entity, BN on 1 October 20X0. Goodwill arising on the acquisition was $15,000

☐ GHK purchased a brand name from a competitor on 1 November 20X0, for $65,000

☐ GHK spent $21,000 during the year on the development of a new product. The product is being launched on the market on 1 December 20X1 and is expected to be profitable

8.3 In its first year of trading to 31 July 20X6, Camp Co incurred the following expenditure on research and development, none of which related to the cost of non-current assets: $12,000 on successfully devising processes for converting seaweed into chemicals X, Y and Z and $60,000 on developing a headache pill based on chemical Z. No commercial uses have yet been discovered for chemicals X and Y. Commercial production and sales of the headache pill commenced on 1 April 20X6 and are expected to produce steady profitable income during a 5-year period before being replaced. Adequate resources exist to achieve this.

What is the maximum amount of development costs that must be carried forward at 31 July 20X6 under IAS 38 *Intangible assets*?

☐ $48,000
☐ $56,000
☐ $60,000
☐ $72,000

8.4 A whisky distiller incurs the following costs: $38,000 developing new distilling techniques that will be put in place shortly to cut the production cost of making malt whisky; $27,000 researching a new process to improve the quality of standard whisky and $8,000 on market research into the commercial viability of a new type of malt whisky. It is company policy to capitalise costs whenever permitted by IAS 38 *Intangible assets*.

How much should be charged as research and development expenditure in profit or loss? (ignore amortisation)

☐ $73,000
☐ $35,000
☐ $27,000
☐ $38,000

9 Impairment of assets

9.1 **Which of the following would be an *internal* indicator of impairment of a machine, according to IAS 36 *Impairment of Assets*?**

☐ The market value of the machine has fallen significantly

☐ There have been significant changes in the technological environment affecting the business in which the machine is used

☐ The operating performance of the machine has declined

☐ The machine is fully depreciated

9.2 The following values relate to a non-current asset:

(i) Carrying amount $20,000
(ii) Net realisable value $18,000
(iii) Value in use $22,000
(iv) Replacement cost $50,000

What is the recoverable amount of the asset?

☐ $18,000
☐ $20,000
☐ $22,000
☐ $50,000

9.3 BI owns a building which it uses as its offices, warehouse and garage. The land is carried as a separate non-current tangible asset in the statement of financial position.

BI has a policy of regularly revaluing its non-current tangible assets. The original cost of the building in October 20X2 was $1,000,000; it was assumed to have a remaining useful life of 20 years at that date, with no residual value. The building was revalued on 30 September 20X4 by a professional valuer at $1,800,000.

The economic climate had deteriorated during 20X5, causing BI to carry out an impairment review of its assets at 30 September 20X5. BI's building was valued at a market value of $1,500,000 on 30 September 20X5 by an independent valuer.

Calculate the impairment loss suffered at 30 September 20X5 and write in the second box whether it should be recognised as part of BI's profit or loss for the period or in other comprehensive income.

$ [   ] [   ]

9.4 A machine has a carrying amount of $144,000. It could be sold for $133,200 with selling costs of $3,600. Its current replacement cost is $250,000 and its value in use is estimated at $150,000.

In accordance with IAS 36 *Impairment of Assets*, what (if any) is the impairment loss that should be recognised in respect of this machine?

☐ $7,200
☐ $6,000
☐ $13,200
☐ Nil

9.5 DS purchased a machine on 1 October 20X2 at a cost of $21,000. The machine had an expected useful life of six years with no expected residual value. DS depreciates its machines using the straight line basis.

The machine has been used and depreciated for three years to 30 September 20X5. New technology was invented in December 20X5, before the financial statements for the year ended 30 September 20X5 were authorised for issue, which enabled a cheaper, more efficient machine to be produced. The Board of DS have realised that this new technology will make their type of machine obsolete in the next couple of years and have concluded that their machine has a fair value of $9,200 and a value in use of $9,000. Selling costs of $500 would be incurred were DS to sell the machine.

Calculate the impairment loss to be recognised in the financial statements for the year ended 30 September 20X5.

$ [   ]

9.6 NS owns a brand name which it acquired on 1 October 20X0 for $500,000. The brand name is being amortised over 10 years.

During 20X5 the economic climate deteriorated causing NS to carry out an impairment review of its assets at 30 September 20X5.

A brand specialist valued NS's brand name at market value of $200,000 on 30 September 20X5 whilst NS's management accountant calculated that the brand name's value in use at 30 September 20X5 was $150,000.

Calculate the value of the impairment loss relating to the brand at 30 September 20X5.

$ [   ]

10 Reporting financial performance I

10.1   Company X closed one of its divisions 10 months ago. It has yet to dispose of one remaining machine. The carrying amount of the machine at the date when business ceased was $750,000. It was being depreciated at 25% on a reducing balance basis. Company X has been advised that the fair value of the machine is $740,000 and expects to incur costs of $10,000 in making the sale. It has located a probable buyer but the sale will not be completed before the year end.

At what amount should the machine be shown in the year end financial statements of Company X?

☐ $562,500
☐ $730,000
☐ $740,000
☐ $750,000

10.2   Company Y closed one of its divisions 9 months ago. It has yet to dispose of one remaining machine. The carrying amount of the machine at the date when business ceased was $600,000 and it was being depreciated at 20% on a reducing balance basis. Company Y has been advised that the fair value of the machine is $610,000 and expects to incur costs of $20,000 in making the sale. It has located a probable buyer but the sale will not be completed before the year end.

Where should the carrying amount of the machine be shown in Company Y's statement of financial position?

☐   Under non-current assets
☐   Under current assets
☐   Included within inventory
☐   Included within receivables

10.3   At its year end of 31 March 20X4 Macey has a machine on hand that it intends to sell in the next few months. It has identified several possible buyers and has priced the machine fairly according to the current market.

How should the machine be accounted for in the financial statements at 31 March 20X4 in accordance with IFRS 5 *Non-current Assets Held for Sale and Discontinued Operations*?

☐   Continue to recognise the machine within property, plant and equipment but no longer depreciate it

☐   Disclose the machine separately from other property, plant and equipment and no longer depreciate it

☐   Continue to recognise the machine within property, plant and equipment and depreciate it

☐   Disclose the machine separately from other property, plant and equipment but continue to depreciate it

10.4   Costcom sold all its branches in North America during 20X2.

How should the results of its North American venture be shown in the statement of profit or loss for the year ended 31 December 20X2?

☐   No separate presentation, all amounts included in standard headings, but disclosure in the notes

☐   No separate presentation for results of North American operation but separate presentation for any profit or loss on disposal

☐   Results of North American operation shown line-by-line in separate column headed 'discontinued operations'

☐   After tax results of North American operation, including any profit or loss on disposal, shown as a one-line entry 'profit/ loss from discontinued operation'

10.5 BJ is an entity based in Europe that provides a range of facilities for holidaymakers and travellers.

At 1 October 20X4 these included:

- A short haul airline operating within Europe; and
- A travel agency specialising in arranging holidays to more exotic destinations, such as Hawaii and Fiji.

BJ's airline operation has made significant losses for the last two years. On 31 January 20X5, the directors of BJ decided that, due to a significant increase in competition on short haul flights within Europe, BJ would close all of its airline operations and dispose of its fleet of aircraft. All flights for holiday makers and travellers who had already booked seats would be provided by third party airlines. All operations ceased on 31 May 20X5.

On 31 July 20X5, BJ sold its fleet of aircraft and associated non-current assets for $500 million; the carrying amount at that date was $750 million.

At the reporting date, BJ were still in negotiation with some employees regarding severance payments. BJ has estimated that in the financial period October 20X5 to September 20X6, they will agree a settlement of $20 million compensation. The airline operation made a loss for the year ended 30 September 20X5 of $100 million.

The closure of the airline operation caused BJ to carry out a major restructuring of the entire entity. The restructuring has been agreed by the directors and active steps have been taken to implement it. The cost of restructuring to be incurred in year 20X5/20X6 is estimated at $10 million.

Calculate the loss that should be disclosed on the statement of profit or loss and other comprehensive income for the year ended 30 September 20X5 assuming that BJ makes the minimum disclosure required in relation to IFRS 5 *Non-current assets held for sale and discontinued operations*.

$ _____

10.6 **Which TWO of the following criteria need NOT be satisfied in order for a division to be classified as "held for sale" in accordance with IFRS 5: *Non-current assets held for sale and discontinued operations*?**

☐ It must be available for immediate sale in its present condition
☐ The sale must be highly probable
☐ Management must be committed to selling it
☐ The sale price must be at at least its fair value
☐ The sale must have been agreed at the end of the reporting period but need not have been completed

---

10.7 MN has a year-end of 31 of March and operates a number of retail outlets around the country. One retail outlet was closed on 31 March 20X1 when trading ceased and the outlet was put up for sale. The directors are certain that the outlet meets the requirements of IFRS 5 *Non-current Assets Held for Sale and Discontinued Operations* for treatment as non-current assets held for sale.

The carrying amounts of the property, plant and equipment held by the discontinued operation on 1 April 20X0 were as follows:

Asset type	Cost-discontinued operations $'000	Accumulated depreciation-discontinued operations $'000	Carrying amount $'000
Land	150	0	150
Buildings	40	20	20
Plant and Equipment	60	35	25
	250	55	195

MN depreciates buildings at 5% per annum on the straight-line basis and plant and equipment at 20% per annum using the reducing balance method.

The fair value less cost to sell of the assets of the closed retail outlet at 31 March 20X1 was $176,000.

Calculate the impairment loss on the assets of the closed retail outlet on 31 March 20X1 when they were classified as held for sale.

$ [   ]

10.8 On 1 October 20X3 Pumpkin changed its production process and one of its machines was no longer required and was offered for sale. At the year end of 31 December 20X3 several buyers were interested but no sale had yet taken place. The machine cost $600,000 at 1 January 20X0 and was being depreciated on a straight line basis over 10 years. At 31 December 20X3 it was estimated to have a fair value less costs of disposal of $400,000 and a value in use of $350,000.

At what amount should the machine be presented in the statement of financial position of Pumpkin at 31 December 20X3?

- ☐ $400,000
- ☐ $350,000
- ☐ $360,000
- ☐ $375,000

10.9 **Which of the following must be disclosed on the face of the statement of profit or loss prepared under IFRS 5 for discontinued activities?**

- ☐ Profit or loss after tax, including gain or loss on disposal
- ☐ Revenue and profit after tax
- ☐ Revenue, expenses and pre tax profit
- ☐ Revenue, costs of sales and operating profit

10.10 **Under IFRS 5, which TWO of the following are NOT factors in an operation being treated as a discontinued activity in the financial statements?**

- ☐ Sale or closure must be completed by the end of the reporting period
- ☐ It represents a separate line of business
- ☐ The anticipated sale is an associate acquired exclusively with a view to resale
- ☐ The sale or closure is part of a single co-ordinated plan to dispose of a major line of business

---

11 Reporting financial performance II

11.1 **Which TWO of the following statements, in respect of foreign currency translation, are correct according to IAS 21 *The effects of changes in foreign exchange rates*?**

- ☐ The functional currency of an entity is selected by management
- ☐ The presentation currency of an entity is selected by management
- ☐ The functional currency of an entity is identified by reference to circumstances of the business
- ☐ The presentation currency of an entity is identified by reference to circumstances of the business

---

11.2 **Where an entity has under-estimated the amount of tax due in the previous year, the under-provision should be:**

- ☐ Paid to the tax authorities this year
- ☐ Added to the current tax payable in the statement of financial position
- ☐ Added to the tax expense in the statement of profit or loss
- ☐ Ignored

11.3 In the year to 31 March 20X8 Company Z made taxable profits of $800,000 on which company tax is payable at 30%. In the previous year corporate income tax had been estimated as $210,000, but was subsequently agreed at $226,000 with the tax authorities.

What are the figures for tax in the statement of profit or loss and tax payable in the statement of financial position at 31 March 20X8?

- ☐ Statement of profit or loss: $224,000; Statement of financial position $240,000
- ☐ Statement of profit or loss: $256,000; Statement of financial position $226,000
- ☐ Statement of profit or loss: $224,000; Statement of financial position $256,000
- ☐ Statement of profit or loss: $256,000; Statement of financial position $240,000

11.4 DT's final dividend for the year ended 31 October 20X5 of $150,000 was declared on 1 February 20X6 and paid in cash on 1 April 20X6. The financial statements were approved on 31 March 20X6.

Which TWO of the following statements reflect the correct treatment of the dividend?

- ☐ The payment clears an accrued liability set up as at 31 October 20X5

- ☐ The dividend is shown as a deduction in the statement of profit or loss and other comprehensive income for the year ended 31 October 20X6

- ☐ The dividend is shown as an accrued liability as at 31 October 20X6

- ☐ The $150,000 dividend was shown in the notes to the financial statements at 31 October 20X5

- ☐ The dividend is shown as a deduction in the statement of changes in equity for the year ended 31 October 20X6

11.5 **Which of the following statements about IAS 10 *Events after the reporting period* are correct?**

- ☐ A material event that occurs before the financial statements are authorised that provides more evidence of conditions that already existed at the reporting date should be adjusted for in the financial statements

- ☐ The notes to the financial statements must give details of non-adjusting events affecting the users' ability to understand the company's financial position

- ☐ Financial statements should not be prepared on a going concern basis if after the end of the reporting period but before the financial statements are authorised the directors have decided to liquidate the company

11.6 **Which TWO of the following statements is correct regarding the restatement of foreign currency assets and liabilities in the financial statements of a single entity at the reporting date?**

- ☐ Non-monetary assets and all long term liabilities should not be restated
- ☐ Monetary assets and liabilities should be restated at the average rate for the period
- ☐ Monetary assets and liabilities should be restated at the closing rate
- ☐ Non-monetary assets and liabilities should not be restated

11.7 A company had a credit balance brought forward on current tax of $20,000. During the year it paid tax of $18,000 and it has a provision for the current year of $50,000.

What is the total charge to tax for the year in the statement of profit or loss?

- ☐ $20,000
- ☐ $48,000
- ☐ $50,000
- ☐ $52,000

11.8 A company had a debit balance brought forward on current tax of $2,000. During the year it has paid no tax and received a tax refund of $1,800. It has a provision for the current year of $30,000.

What is the total charge to tax for the year in the statement of profit or loss?

☐ $29,800
☐ $30,000
☐ $30,200
☐ $32,000

11.9 A company's statement of profit or loss and other comprehensive income showed a profit before tax of $1,800,000.

After the year end and before the financial statements were authorised for issue, the following events took place.

(1)   The value of an investment held at the year end fell by $85,000.

(2)   A customer who owed $116,000 at the year end went bankrupt.

(3)   Inventory valued at cost of $161,000 in the statement of financial position was sold for $141,000.

(4)   Assets with a carrying amount at the year end of $240,000 were unexpectedly seized by the local government.

What is the company's profit after making the necessary adjustments for these events?

☐ $1,399,000
☐ $1,579,000
☐ $1,664,000
☐ $1,800,000

11.10 GD's financial reporting period is 1 September 20X7 to 31 August 20X8.

Assuming that all amounts are material and that GD's financial statements have not yet been approved for publication, which one of the following would be classified as a non-adjusting event according to IAS 10 *Events after the reporting period*?

☐   On 30 October 20X8, GD received a communication stating that one of its customers had ceased trading and gone into liquidation. The balance outstanding at 31 August 20X8 was unlikely to be paid

☐   At 31 August 20X8, GD had not provided for an outstanding legal action against the local government administration for losses suffered as a result of incorrect enforcement of local business regulations. On 5 November 20X8, the court awarded GD $50,000 damages

☐   On 1 October 20X8, GD made a rights issue of 1 new share for every 3 shares held at a price of $175. The market price on that date was $200

☐   At 31 August 20X8, GD had an outstanding insurance claim of $150,000. On 10 October 20X8, the insurance company informed GD that it would pay $140,000 as settlement

12 Employee benefits

12.1 **Which of the following statements about IAS 19 *Employee Benefits* is correct?**

☐ IAS 19 applies only to companies whose shares are publicly traded

☐ IAS 19 requires that an independent actuarial valuation of defined benefit liability is undertaken every year

☐ IAS 19 requires all re-measurement gains and losses each year to be reported in other comprehensive income

☐ IAS 19 requires all re-measurement gains and losses each year to be reported in profit or loss

12.2 **Which ONE of the following statements are true about the operation of a typical defined contribution scheme?**

☐ The role of the actuary is critical in determining the pension liability
☐ Companies sometimes take holidays from making their contributions
☐ Once they have paid their contributions the company's liability is met
☐ There is almost certain to be a statement of financial position asset or liability at the end of the year

12.3 **Which of the following options is a characteristic of a defined benefit pension scheme?**

☐ The pension payable to an employee is calculated by reference to the salary earned in the qualifying period prior to retirement

☐ The pension fund is built up by employee and employer contributions and will be guaranteed to fund the pension commitments eventually

☐ The cost of the provision of pensions to the employer is a fixed, known amount

☐ The statement of profit or loss charge for pension costs reflects the payment into the fund

12.4 DEF operates a defined contribution pension scheme and contributes 6% of employees' total remuneration into this pension scheme each year.

During the year ended 30 June 20X2 a total of $20 million was paid in salaries. A bonus of $6 million was paid in August 20X2 based on the profit for the year ended 30 June 20X2.

DEF had paid $950,000 into the plan by 30 June 20X2.

What will be the accrual in the statement of financial position at 30 June 20X2?

☐ $950,000
☐ $250,000
☐ $610,000
☐ $1,200,000

12.5 **Which of the following correctly identifies the defined benefit expense that is recognised in the statement of profit or loss?**

☐ Current service cost + net interest on net defined asset/liability + past service cost
☐ Current service cost + net interest on net defined asset/liability + contributions paid
☐ Current service cost + net interest on net defined asset/liability + re-measurement gains/losses
☐ Current service cost + net interest on net defined asset/liability – benefits paid to former employees

BPP
LEARNING MEDIA

12.6 **Which TWO of the following are terms used to define pension schemes as identified by IAS 19 Employee Benefits?**

☐ Money purchase scheme
☐ Defined contribution scheme
☐ Company pension scheme
☐ Defined benefit scheme

12.7 XYZ operates a defined benefit pension plan for its employees. The present value of the plan's obligations on 1 September 20X4 was $6,600,000 increasing to $7,200,000 by the entity's year end on 31 August 20X5. Benefits paid to members of the pension plan during the year were $650,000 and the current service cost for the financial year was $875,000. The increase in the present value of the pension plan's liabilities for the year was $540,000.

What was the re-measurement gain or loss in respect of the plan's obligations for the year ended 31 August 20X5?

$ [   ]

12.8 ASD operates a defined benefit pension plan. At 1 January 20X2 the fair value of the pension plan assets was $5,700,000.

The actuary estimates that the service cost for the year ended 31 December 20X2 is $1,020,000 and the relevant discount rate was 4% for the year ended 31 December 20X2. The pension plan paid $280,000 to retired members and ASD paid $820,000 in contributions to the pension plan for the year ended 31 December 20X2.

At 31 December 20X2 the re-measurement loss on the plan assets was $168,000.

What is the fair value of the pension plan assets at 31 December 20X2?

☐ $6,636,000
☐ $6,300,000
☐ $7,320,000
☐ $5,816,000

12.9 GH operates a defined benefit pension plan. At 1 April 20X2 the fair value of the pension plan assets was $2,700,000 and the present value of the pension plan obligations was $3,000,000.

The service cost for the year ended 31 March 20X3 was $650,000. The relevant discount rate for the year ended 31 March 20X3 was estimated at 5% and GH paid $950,000 in contributions to the plan.

The pension plan paid $320,000 to retired members in the year ended 31 March 20X3.

At 31 March 20X3 the fair value of the pension plan assets was $3,600,000 and the present value of the plan obligations was $3,800,000.

How much is the expense in the statement of profit or loss for the year ended 31 March 20X3?

☐ $1,615,000
☐ $800,000
☐ $665,000
☐ $650,000

12.10 Which one of the following statements would cause a re-measurement gain or loss?

☐ A change in the rules of a pension scheme granting additional benefits to existing pensioners

☐ A change in the contributions paid into the scheme

☐ Payment of pensions to former employees

☐ A change in the actuarial assumptions in respect of the valuation of the present value of the pension plan's obligations

13 Statement of cashflows

13.1 In a statement of cash flows which of the following would NOT be shown as a cash flow within the 'cash flows from financing' section?

☐ Issue of ordinary shares
☐ Repurchase of a long-term loan
☐ Dividends paid
☐ Repayment of an overdraft

13.2 Which one of the items below would NOT appear in the statement of cash flows?

☐ Cash receipts from customers
☐ Dividend paid to preference shareholders in the year
☐ Repayment of a bank loan
☐ The statement of profit or loss charge for taxation for the current year

13.3 In a company's statement of cash flows, a revaluation of non-current assets during the year will be:

☐ Shown as an adjustment to profit before tax
☐ Shown as a cash inflow
☐ Disclosed under investing activities
☐ Entirely excluded

13.4 In a statement of cash flows which of the items below would NOT appear as a cash outflow?

☐ The nominal value of loan notes redeemed at par during the year
☐ The dividends paid to preference shareholders during the year
☐ The statement of profit or loss charge for depreciation for the year
☐ The purchase of long-term investments

13.5 The following balances appear in the statement of financial position of Peterson Co.

Year ending 31 October

	20X4	20X3
	$'000	$'000
Share capital	1,600	1,200
Share premium	400	280

What figure would appear in the statement of cash flows for the proceeds from the issue of shares? Answer to the nearest $'000.

$ [   ] ('000)

13.6   At 1 October 20X4, BK had a balance of accrued interest payable amounting to $12,000.

During the year ended 30 September 20X5, BK charged interest payable of $41,000 to its statement of profit of loss and other comprehensive income.

The closing balance on accrued interest payable account at 30 September 20X5 was $15,000.

How much interest paid should BK show on its statement of cash flows for the year ended 30 September 20X5?

☐ $38,000
☐ $41,000
☐ $44,000
☐ $53,000

13.7   A statement of cash flows shows the increase or decrease in cash and cash equivalents in the period.

Which THREE of the following items are included in this movement?

☐   Cash at bank

☐   Bank overdraft

☐   Current asset investments readily convertible into known amounts of cash and which can be sold without disrupting the company's business

☐   Equity investments

13.8   **Which THREE of the following items should NOT appear in a company's statement of cash flows?**

☐   Proposed dividends
☐   Dividends received
☐   Bonus issue of shares
☐   Surplus on revaluation of a non-current asset
☐   Proceeds of sale of an investment not connected with the company's trading activities

13.9   **Which one of the following would need to be deducted from profit before tax in order to generate a figure for net cash from operating activities?**

☐   Amortisation charge for the year
☐   Surplus on revaluation of property
☐   Capital element of a loan repayment
☐   Profit on sale of a non-current asset

13.10   Blacksmith disposes of an asset with a carrying amount of $21,000 for $30,000 on 7 July 20X1.

How will this transaction be disclosed in the statement of cash flows using the indirect method?

☐   Cash flows from operating activities reconciliation: $(9,000); Cash inflow: $30,000
☐   Cash flows from operating activities reconciliation: $9,000; Cash inflow: $30,000
☐   Cash flows from operating activities reconciliation: $(21,000); Cash inflow: $30,000
☐   Cash flows from operating activities reconciliation: $21,000; Cash inflow: $30,000

14 The consolidated statement of financial position I

14.1 On 1 January 20X5 Plane acquired 60% of the equity share capital of Sycamore. Goodwill of $100,000 arose on the acquisition.

Sycamore's performance for the years ended 31 December 20X5 and 31 December 20X6 slightly exceeded budget. However, in the year ended 31 December 20X7 it made substantial losses that had not been forecast.

The goodwill arising on the acquisition of Sycamore should be reviewed for impairment:

- ☐ Annually
- ☐ In 20X5
- ☐ In 20X7
- ☐ In 20X5 and 20X7

14.2 **Which ONE of the following is a valid reason for excluding a subsidiary from consolidation under current International Financial Reporting Standards?**

- ☐ The subsidiary has been acquired exclusively with a view to its subsequent disposal

- ☐ The activities of the subsidiary are so dissimilar from those of the rest of the group that it would be misleading to include it in the consolidation

- ☐ A formally documented decision has been made by the directors to wind down the activities of the subsidiary

- ☐ The subsidiary operates in a different country from the parent

14.3 AB acquired 4,000 of the 10,000 equity voting shares and 8,000 of the 10,000 non-voting preference shares in CD.

AB acquired 4,000 of the 10,000 equity voting shares in EF and had a signed agreement giving it the power to appoint or remove all of the directors of EF.

Which investment would be classified as a subsidiary of AB?

- ☐ Both CD and EF
- ☐ CD Only
- ☐ EF Only
- ☐ Neither CD or EF

14.4 VZ acquired 75% of KY on 1 July 20X2 when KY's retained earnings were $65,000.

Goodwill of $48,000 arose on acquisition. An impairment review was undertaken at 30 June 20X3 and the goodwill was found to be impaired by $10,000.

It is the group policy to value non-controlling interest at fair value of net assets at acquisition which was $14,800.

KY's retained earnings on 30 June 20X3 had risen to $115,000.

Calculate the value of the non-controlling interest at 30 June 20X3 for inclusion in the consolidated statement of financial position.

$ ☐

14.5 VZ acquired 75% of KY on 1 July 20X2 when KY's share capital and retained earnings were $310,000 and $165,000 respectively.

Goodwill of $148,000 arose on acquisition. An impairment review was undertaken at 30 June 20X3 and the goodwill was found to be impaired by $100,000.

It is the group policy to value non-controlling interest at the proportionate share of net assets.

KY's retained earnings on 30 June 20X3 had risen to $215,000.

What is the value of the non-controlling interest at 30 June 20X3 for inclusion in the consolidated statement of financial position?

- ☐ $131,250
- ☐ $106,250
- ☐ $172,500
- ☐ $156,250

14.6 Goodwill arising on acquisition is accounted for according to IFRS 3 *Business combinations*.

Which statement is correct concerning the accounting treatment of goodwill arising on acquisition?

- ☐   Carried at cost, with an annual impairment review
- ☐   Written off against reserves on acquisition
- ☐   Amortised over its useful life
- ☐   Revalued to fair value at each year end

14.7 LM acquired 60% of VB on 1 April 20X7 for $6.4 million when VB's retained earnings were $2.3 million.

An extract from the statement of financial position for both entities for the year ended 31 March 20X9 is:

	LM $'m	VB $'m
Share capital	5.5	4.4
Retained Earnings	8.5	3.2
	14	7.6

It is the group policy to value non-controlling interest at acquisition at the proportionate share of net assets. There has been no impairment of the goodwill arising at acquisition.

What is the value of the non-controlling interest for inclusion in the statement of financial position at 31 March 20X9?

- ☐ $2.68 million
- ☐ $3.04 million
- ☐ $8.1 million
- ☐ $3.96 million

14.8 DS acquired 90% of LO on 1 January 20X1 for $22.8 million when LO's retained earnings were $6.3 million.

Extracts from the statement of financial position of both entities at 31 December 20X1 are:

	DS $'m	LO $'m
Share capital	55.8	12.6
Retained Earnings	42.6	7.9
	98.4	20.5

It is the group policy to value non-controlling interest at fair value at the date of acquisition which was $2.3 million.

There has been no impairment of the goodwill arising at acquisition.

What is the value of the non-controlling interest at 31 December 20X1 for the consolidated statement of financial position?

$ [   ] million

14.9   TR acquired 70% of SD on 1 September 20X5. At this date the equity of SD comprised:

	$'m
$1 equity shares	90
Retained earnings	63
Revaluation surplus	32

The equity sections of the statement of financial position for both TR and SD at the 31 August 20X9 are:

	TR	SD
	$'m	$'m
$ 1 equity shares	216	90
Retained earnings	142	63
Revaluation surplus	81	54

What is the value of the revaluation surplus in the consolidated statement of financial position at 31 August 20X9?

☐ $15.4 million
☐ $96.4 million
☐ $118.8 million
☐ $238.4 million

14.10   QZ acquired 80% of the share capital of FT on 1 January 20X9 for $350,000.

The equity sections of the statement of financial position of both companies at 31 December 20X9 are:

	QZ	FT
	$	$
Issued share capital - $1 shares	400,000	140,000
Share premium account	320,000	50,000
Retained earnings at 1 January 20X9	140,000	60,000
Profit for the year ended 31 December 20X9	80,000	40,000
	940,000	290,000

Goodwill of $240,000 arose on acquisition. An impairment loss of $36,000 had arisen at the year ending 31 December 20X9.

It is the group policy to value non-controlling interest at the fair value of the net assets at acquisition.

What figure for consolidated retained earnings should appear in the consolidated statement of financial position at 31 December 20X9?

☐ $143,200
☐ $216,000
☐ $223,200
☐ $271,200

---

15 The consolidated statement of financial position II

15.1 DA owns 60% of CB's ordinary share capital. At the group's year end, 31 December 20X5, CB included $6,000 in its receivables in respect of goods supplied to DA. However, the payables of DA included only $4,000 in respect of amounts due to CB. The difference arose because, on 31 December 20X5, DA sent a cheque for $2,000, which was not received by CB until 3 January 20X6.

Which ONE of the following sets of consolidation adjustments to current assets and current liabilities is correct?

☐ Deduct $6,000 from both consolidated receivables and consolidated payables

☐ Deduct $3,600 from both consolidated receivables and consolidated payables

☐ Deduct $6,000 from consolidated receivables and $4,000 from consolidated payables, and include cash in transit of $2,000

☐ Deduct $6,000 from consolidated receivables and $4,000 from consolidated payables, and include inventory in transit of $2,000

15.2 C acquired 75% of G on 1 April 20X3 when G's retained earnings were $370,000. The group policy is to value non-controlling interest at fair value of net assets which were $48,000.

G sold a piece of machinery to C on 1 April 20X4 for $115,000 which had been included in G's accounts for a carrying amount of $90,000. The machine has a remaining useful life of 5 years on 1 April 20X4.

Calculate the value of the non-controlling interest to be included in the consolidated statement of financial position for the year ending 31 March 20X5 assuming G's retained earnings on 31 March 20X5 were $520,000.

$ [   ]

15.3 YZ acquired 80% of WX on 1 October 20X2.

YZ and WX trade with each other. During the year ended 30 September 20X3 YZ sold WX inventory at a sales price of $28,000. YZ applied a mark up on cost of 33⅓%.

At 30 September 20X3 WX still had remaining in inventory $6,000 of goods purchased from YZ.

Which of the following is the correct journal entry to be made to adjust YZ's consolidated statement of financial position for the year ended 30 September 20X3?

☐ Dr Retained earnings of YZ $1,500, Cr Consolidated inventory $1,500
☐ Dr Retained earnings of WX $1,500, Cr Consolidated inventory $1,500
☐ Dr Retained earnings of YZ $2,000, Cr Consolidated inventory $2,000
☐ Dr Retained earnings of WX $2,000, Cr Consolidated inventory $2,000

15.4 BV acquired 75% of JK on 1 May 20X6.

The retained earnings in the financial statements of BV and JK as at 31 December 20X6 are $2,560,000 and $880,000 respectively. JK made a profit for the year of $144,000.

There has been no impairment to the goodwill since acquisition.

What are the consolidated retained earnings for inclusion in the consolidated statement of financial position of the BV group as at 31 December 20X6?

☐ $2,623,000
☐ $2,632,000
☐ $2,641,000
☐ $3,220,000

15.5 XY owns 80% of the issued share capital of PQ.

During the current accounting period XY sells goods to PQ for $7.8 million, the goods cost $6.5 million. XY achieved a mark up on cost of 20%. Half of the goods remain in PQ's inventory at the year end.

Which of the following is the correct treatment of this transaction when preparing the consolidated financial statements?

☐ Remove $7.8 million from revenue and cost of sales. Increase cost of sales and reduce inventory by the profit on the goods remaining in inventory at the year end

☐ Increase cost of sales and reduce inventory by the profit on the goods remaining in inventory at the year end

☐ Remove $7.8 million from revenue and $6.5 million from cost of sales. Increase cost of sales and reduce inventory by the profit on the goods remaining in inventory at the year end

☐ Remove $6.5 million from revenue and cost of sales. Increase cost of sales and reduce inventory by the profit on the goods remaining in inventory at the year end

15.6 LPD buys goods from its 75% owned subsidiary QPR. QPR earns a mark-up of 25% on such transactions. At the group's year end, 30 June 20X7, LPD had not yet taken delivery of goods, at a sales value of $100,000, which were despatched by QPR on 29 June 20X7.

At what amount would the goods in transit appear in the consolidated statement of financial position sheet of the LPD group at 30 June 20X7?

☐ $60,000
☐ $75,000
☐ $80,000
☐ $100,000

15.7 STV owns 75% of the ordinary share capital of its subsidiary TUW. At the group's year end, 28 February 20X7, STV's payables include $3,600 in respect of inventories sold to it by TUW.

TUW's receivables include $6,700 in respect of inventories sold to STV. Two days before the year end STV sent a payment of $3,100 to TUW that was not recorded by the latter until two days after the year end.

How should the in-transit item be dealt with in the consolidated statement of financial position at 28 February 20X7?

☐ $2,325 to be included as cash in transit
☐ $3,100 to be added to consolidated payables
☐ $3,100 to be included as inventories in transit
☐ $3,100 to be included as cash in transit

15.8 A parent company sells inventory costing $100,000 at a mark up of 20% to a 90% subsidiary. At the end of the reporting period half of this inventory remains unsold.

Which one of the following is the required consolidation adjustment?

☐ Reduce group inventory by $100,000 as the sale was not made to a third party

☐ No adjustment is needed because intra group trading cancels on consolidation

☐ Reduce group inventory by $10,000 and reduce parent's profits by $10,000 to eliminate the unrealised profit in inventory

☐ Reduce group inventory by $10,000 and subsidiary's profits by $10,000 to eliminate the unrealised profit in inventory

15.9 X Co transfers an asset which had a cost of $10,000 to its 80% owned subsidiary Y Co in 20X1. The transfer price was $17,000. Both companies charge straight line depreciation at 10% p.a. A full year's charge is made in the year of acquisition and none in the year of transfer/disposal.

X Co had owned the asset for 5 years prior to the transfer. The asset had a remaining useful life of 5 years at the date of sale.

What is the net adjustment required to group profit?

$ [   ]

15.10 MX acquired 80% of FZ on 1 January 20X9 when FZ's retained earnings were $920,000.

FZ sold goods to MX at a sales value of $300,000. All of these goods remain in MX's inventories at the year end. FZ makes 20% profit margin on all sales.

The retained earnings of MX and FZ as at 31 December 20X9 are $3.2 million and $1.1 million respectively. There has been no impairment to goodwill since the date of acquisition.

What amount will appear in the consolidated statement of financial position of the MX group for retained earnings as at 31 December 20X9?

☐ $3,284,000
☐ $3,296,000
☐ $3,304,000
☐ $4,032,000

16 The consolidated statement of profit of loss and other comprehensive income

16.1 Pumpkin has held 90% of the equity share capital of Squash for many years. Cost of sales for each entity for the year ended 31 December 20X3 was as follows:

	$
Pumpkin	100,000
Squash	80,000

During the year, Squash sold goods costing $5,000 to Pumpkin for $8,000. At the year end, all these goods remained in inventory.

What figure should be shown as cost of sales in the consolidated statement of profit or loss of the Pumpkin group for the year ended 31 December 20X3?

☐ $178,000
☐ $177,000
☐ $175,000
☐ $183,000

16.2 GPT regularly sells goods to its subsidiary in which it owns 60% of the ordinary share capital. During the group's financial year ended 31 August 20X7, GPT sold goods to its subsidiary valued at $100,000 (selling price) upon which it makes a margin of 20%. By the group's year end all of the goods had been sold to parties outside the group.

What is the correct consolidation adjustment in respect of these sales for the year ended 31 August 20X7?

- ☐ No adjustment required
- ☐ Dr Revenue $60,000; Cr Cost of sales $60,000
- ☐ Dr Revenue $80,000; Cr Cost of sales $80,000
- ☐ Dr Revenue $100,000; Cr Cost of sales $100,000

16.3 YZ purchased 80% of the equity shares in WX on 1 October 20X2.

YZ and WX trade with each other. During the year ended 30 September 20X3 YZ sold WX inventory at a sales price of $28,000. YZ applied a mark up on cost of 33⅓%.

At 30 September 2013 WX still had remaining in inventory $6,000 of the goods purchased from YZ.

Select the correct values and narratives from the lists and complete the two journal entries to make the required adjustments in YZ's consolidated statement of profit and loss for the year ended 30 September 20X3 for the above.

	Dr	Cr
Group revenue	☐	
☐		☐
Being removal of intra group trading		
☐	☐	
Group inventory		☐
Being removal unrealised profit		
Group cost of sales	28,000	
Group gross profit	21,000	
WX cost of sales	1,500	
YZ cost of sales	2,000	

16.4 AB acquired a 60% holding in CD many years ago. At 31 December 20X3 AB held inventory with a book value of $30,000 purchased from CD at cost plus 20%.

The effect on the consolidated statement of profit or loss for the year is:

	Group Profit	Non-controlling interest
☐	Reduced by $3,000	Reduced by $2,000
☐	Reduced by $3,600	Reduced by $2,400
☐	Reduced by $5,000	No effect
☐	Reduced by $6,000	No effect

16.5 DS acquired 80% of AQ on 1 October 20X7.

The statement of profit or loss for both companies for the year ended 30 September 20X8 is as follows:

	DS $	AQ $
Revenue	8,700	3,600
Cost of sales and expenses	(2,400)	(1,700)
Profit before tax	6,300	1,900
Income tax expense	(1,700)	(800)
Profit for the year	4,600	1,100

It is the group policy to value non-controlling interest at fair value of net assets acquired at acquisition. The goodwill arising at acquisition was $4,200 and an impairment loss for the year ended 30 September 20X8 of $600 arose.

The profit attributable to the non-controlling interest for the year ended 30 September 20X8 is:

☐ $100
☐ $220
☐ $380
☐ $5,000

16.6 ZA acquired 70% of MB on 1 January 20X7.

An extract from their respective statement of profit or loss for the year ended 31 December 20X7 is as follows:

	ZA $'000	MB $'000
Profit for the year	7,020	1,980

It is the group policy to value non-controlling interest at the proportionate share of the net assets at acquisition. Goodwill of $7,560,000 arose at acquisition and the impairment loss of the current year is $756,000.

The profit attributable to the owner of the parent is:

☐ $846,000
☐ $7,650,000
☐ $7,877,000
☐ $9,162,000

---

17 Associates

17.1 Consul owns the following equity shareholdings in other entities:

Admiral	25%
Sultan	20%
Warrior	30%

Consul has a seat on the board of each entity. Consul is the largest shareholding in Admiral (no other shareholdings are larger than 10%).

Another entity owns 25% of the equity shares in Sultan and also has a seat on its board. No other individual or entity owns more than 5% of the equity share capital of Sultan.

Another entity holds 70% of Warrior's equity and has a seat on its board.

Which entities are associates of Consul?

- ☐ Admiral only
- ☐ Admiral and Sultan
- ☐ Admiral and Warrior
- ☐ Admiral, Sultan and Warrior

17.2 AB acquired 25% of the ordinary share capital of EF on 1 October 20X8.

EF sold goods to AB on 1 May 20X9 with a sales value of $80,000. Half of these goods remained in AB's inventories at the year end. EF makes 25% profit margin on all sales.

EF's profit for the year ended 30 June 20X9 was $100,000.

What is the share of profit of associate for inclusion in the consolidated statement of profit or loss for the year ended 30 June 20X9?

- ☐ $16,250
- ☐ $16,750
- ☐ $18,750
- ☐ $22,500

17.3 Savoy owns 80% of Spring and 30% of White.

Extracts from the statements of profit or loss for the year ended 31 October 20X5:

	Savoy $'000	Spring $'000	White $'000
Profit for the period	700	550	500

What is group profit for the period for the year ended 31 October 20X5?

- ☐ $1,250,000
- ☐ $1,290,000
- ☐ $1,400,000
- ☐ $1,750,000

17.4 R owns 30% of E. During the year ended 31 December 20X8 E sold goods to R for $160,000. E applies a one-third mark up on cost. R still had 25% of these goods in inventory at the year end.

What amount should be deducted from consolidated retained earnings in respect of this transaction?

- ☐ $40,000
- ☐ $3,000
- ☐ $10,000
- ☐ $4,000

---

18 General principles of taxation

18.1   Which of the following statements is correct?

☐   Tax evasion is legally arranging affairs so as to minimise the tax liability. Tax avoidance is the illegal manipulation of the tax system to avoid paying taxes due

☐   Tax evasion is legally arranging affairs so as to evade paying tax. Tax avoidance is tax planning, legally arranging affairs so as to minimise the tax liability

☐   Tax evasion is using loop holes in legislation to evade paying tax. Tax avoidance is the illegal manipulation of the tax system to avoid paying taxes due

☐   Tax evasion is the illegal manipulation of the tax system to avoid paying taxes due. Tax avoidance is tax planning, legally arranging affairs so as to minimise the tax liability

18.2   Which ONE of the following defines the meaning of "tax gap"?

☐   The difference between the tax an entity expects to pay and the amount notified by the tax authority

☐   The difference between the total amount of tax due to be paid and the amount actually collected by the tax authority

☐   The difference between the due date for tax payment and the date it is actually paid

☐   The difference between the amount of tax provided in the financial statements and the amount actually paid

18.3   An ideal tax system should conform to certain principles.

Which one of the following statements is NOT generally regarded as a principle of an ideal tax?

☐   It should be fair to different individuals and should reflect a person's ability to pay
☐   It should not be arbitrary, it should be certain
☐   It should raise as much money as possible for the government
☐   It should be convenient in terms of timing and payment

18.4   Which one of the following powers is a tax authority LEAST likely to have granted to them?

☐   Power of arrest
☐   Power to examine records
☐   Power of entry and search
☐   Power to give information to another country's tax authorities

18.5   Which of the following is LEAST likely to be a reason for governments to set deadlines for filing returns and paying taxes?

☐   To help tax payers know when to pay their taxes
☐   To enable the tax authority to forecast its cash flow more accurately
☐   To provide a reference point for penalties for late payment
☐   To ensure tax is paid early

18.6   Which TWO of the following are MOST LIKELY to encourage an increase in the incidence of tax avoidance or tax evasion?

☐   High penalties for any tax evasion
☐   Imprecise and vague tax laws
☐   A tax system that is seen as fair to everyone
☐   Very high tax rates

18.7 B buys goods from a wholesaler, paying the price of the goods plus VAT (sales tax). B sells goods in its shop to customers. The customers pay the price of the goods plus VAT (sales tax).

From the perspective of B, the VAT (sales tax) would have:

- ☐ Effective incidence
- ☐ Formal incidence
- ☐ Ineffective incidence
- ☐ Informal incidence

18.8 Which of the following BEST describes the effective incidence of a tax?

- ☐ The date the tax is actually paid
- ☐ The person or entity that finally bears the cost of the tax
- ☐ The date the tax assessment is issued
- ☐ The person or entity receiving the tax assessment

18.9 Which ONE of the following powers is not available to tax authorities?

- ☐ Power to review and query filed returns
- ☐ Power to detain company officials
- ☐ Power to request special returns
- ☐ Power to enter and search premises

18.10 Which of the following is the best definition of 'competent jurisdiction' for an entity paying tax?

- ☐ The tax authority that knows the most about the type of taxes the entity pays
- ☐ The tax authority whose tax laws apply to an entity
- ☐ The tax authority in the country where the entity has most of its operations
- ☐ The tax authority which gives the entity the most accurate calculation of taxes payable

19 Direct taxation

19.1 RS purchased an asset on 1 April 20X0 for $375,000, incurring legal fees of $12,000. RS is resident in Country X. There was no indexation allowed on the asset.

RS sold the asset on 31 March 20X3 for $450,000 incurring transaction charges of $15,000.

Relevant tax rules

Corporate profits

The rules for taxation of corporate profits are as follows:

- The corporate tax on profits and capital gains is at a rate of 25%

Calculate the capital gains tax due from RS on disposal of the asset.

Work to the nearest $.

$ ☐

19.2 Which one of the following is NOT a benefit of pay-as-you-earn (PAYE) method of tax collection?

- ☐ It makes payment of tax easier for the tax payer as it is in instalments
- ☐ It makes it easier for governments to forecast tax revenues
- ☐ It benefits the tax payer as it reduces the tax payable
- ☐ It improves governments cash flow as cash is received earlier

19.3 **Which TWO of the following taxes would normally be defined as direct taxation?**

☐ Import duty payable on specific types of imported goods
☐ Individual income tax, usually deducted at source
☐ Corporate income tax
☐ Value added tax

19.4 An entity purchases new computer equipment for $72,000 during the year. The profit for the year (excluding depreciation) was $128,000.

The corporate income tax rate applicable to profits was 25%. The computer equipment qualified for first year tax writing down allowance of 50%.

Calculate the tax payable for the year.

Give your answer to the nearest whole number.

$ ☐☐☐☐☐☐☐

19.5 An entity, resident in country X, had accumulated tax losses of $320,000 at 31 December 20X2. The entity had a taxable profit of $480,000 for the year ended 31 December 20X3.

Relevant tax rules

Corporate profits

The rules for taxation of corporate profits/ losses are as follows:

• Accounting rules on recognition and measurement are followed for tax purposes.
• The corporate tax on profits is at a rate of 25%

Tax losses can be carried forward to offset again future taxable profits from the same business.

For the year ended 31 December 20X3 the entity will:

☐ Pay no tax for the year and carry forward a loss of $200,000
☐ Pay $10,000 tax for the year and have no loss to carry forward
☐ Pay $40,000 tax for the year and have no loss to carry forward
☐ Pay $160,000 tax for the year and have no loss to carry forward

19.6 An entity makes a taxable profit of $600,000 and pays corporate income tax at 25%. The entity pays a dividend to its shareholders. A shareholder, who pays personal tax at 40% receives a $6,000 dividend and then pays an additional $2,400 tax on the dividend.

The tax system could be said to be:

☐ A classical system
☐ An imputation system
☐ A split rate system
☐ A partial imputation system

19.7 An entity, resident in country X, reported accounting profits of $500,000 for the period ended 30 September 20X4. The profit was after deducting entertaining expenses of $51,000 and a donation to a political party of $36,000.

The entity also included a non-taxable government grant receipt of $100,000 in its reported profit.

Relevant tax rules

Corporate profits

The rules for taxation of corporate profits are as follows:

- Accounting rules on recognition and measurement are followed for tax purposes.

- All expenses other than depreciation, amortisation, entertaining, taxes paid to other public bodies and donations to political parties are tax deductible.

- The corporate tax on profits is at a rate of 25%.

Calculate the entity's tax payable for the year ended 30 September 20X4.

Give your answer to the nearest whole number.

$ [   ]

19.8 In Country X a company who is in a member of a group can transfer their trading loss to another group member for offset against its taxable profits. This is called group relief.

Which TWO of the below ARE likely to be advantages of group relief?

☐ It enables tax to be saved at the highest marginal rate
☐ It enables tax to be saved at the highest average rate
☐ It improves the cash flow of the group by enabling the trading loss to be used as soon as possible
☐ It enables more trading loss to be carried forward

19.9 EH is resident in Country X. EH purchased an asset on 1 April 20X2 for $420,000, incurring additional import duties of $30,000. The relevant index increased by 40% in the period from 1 April 20X2 to 31 March 20X9.

EH sold the asset on 31 March 20X9 for $700,000, incurring selling costs of $10,000.

Assume all purchase and selling costs are allowable for tax purposes.

Relevant tax rules

Corporate profits

The rules for taxation of corporate profits are as follows:

- The corporate tax on profits and capital gains is at a rate of 25%

How much tax was due from EH on disposal of its asset?

$ [   ]

19.10 **Relevant tax rules**

An entity purchases an asset, which is eligible for tax depreciation, on 1 January 20X0 for $6,000. The asset is sold for $3,100 on 31 December 20X2.

Corporate profits

Tax depreciation allowances are available on eligible assets at a rate of 50% in the first year and 25% on a reducing balance basis in subsequent years, except for the year of disposal when a balancing charge or allowance will arise.

For the year ended 31 December 20X2 there is a balancing [   ] of $ [   ] .

20 International and indirect taxation

20.1 Which of the following sentences best describes a withholding tax?

- ☐   Tax withheld from payment to the tax authorities
- ☐   Tax paid less an amount withheld from payment
- ☐   Tax deducted at source before payment of interest or dividends
- ☐   Tax paid on increases in value of investment holdings

20.2 Which of the following best describes the purpose of double tax relief?

- ☐   To ensure that you do not pay tax twice on any of your income
- ☐   To mitigate taxing overseas income twice
- ☐   To avoid taxing dividends received from subsidiaries in the same country twice
- ☐   To provide relief where a company pays tax at double the normal rate

20.3 A country has a duty that is levied on all imported petroleum products. This levy is $5 per litre.

This duty could be said to be:

- ☐   General consumption tax
- ☐   Value added tax
- ☐   Specific unit tax
- ☐   Ad valorem tax

20.4 An entity sells household items such as kettles and toasters and adds sales tax to the selling price of all products sold. A customer purchasing the goods has to pay the cost of the goods plus sales tax. The entity pays the sales tax to the tax authority.

Which TWO of the following are appropriate classifications for the sales tax from the perspective of the entity?

- ☐   A direct tax
- ☐   An indirect tax
- ☐   Effective incidence
- ☐   Formal incidence
- ☐   Trading tax

20.5 HY is registered for VAT in Country X.

HY purchased a consignment of goods for $70,000 plus VAT at the standard rate and then sold the goods for $138,000 inclusive of VAT at the standard rate.

Relevant tax rules

Value added tax

Country X has a VAT system which allows entities to reclaim input tax paid.

The country X the VAT rates are:

- Zero rated: 0%
- Standard rated: 15%
- Exempt goods: 0%.

How much profit should HY record in its statement of profit or loss and other comprehensive income for this consignment?

- ☐ $50,000
- ☐ $57,500
- ☐ $68,000
- ☐ $77,130

20.6 Where a resident entity runs an overseas operation as a branch of the entity, certain tax implications arise.

Which ONE of the following does NOT usually apply in relation to an overseas branch?

- ☐ Assets can be transferred to the branch without triggering a capital gain
- ☐ Corporate income tax is paid on profits remitted by the branch
- ☐ Tax depreciation can be claimed on any qualifying assets used in the trade of the branch
- ☐ Losses sustained by the branch are immediately deductible against the resident entity's income

---

20.7 HN purchases products from a foreign country. The products cost $14 each and are subject to excise duty of $3 per item and VAT at the standard rate.

HN is resident in Country X.

Relevant tax rules

Value added tax

Country X has a VAT system which allows entities to reclaim input tax paid.

The country X the VAT rates are:

- Zero rated: 0%
- Standard rated: 15%
- Exempt goods: 0%.

If HN imports 1,000 items, how much does it pay to the tax authorities for this transaction?

- ☐ $2,100
- ☐ $5,100
- ☐ $5,550
- ☐ $19,550

20.8 Ying, a company resident in Country A, is a 100% owned subsidiary of Yang, a company resident in Country B. At the year end, Ying paid a dividend of $80,000 from which withholding tax of $12,000 was deducted, to Yang. Country B charges corporate income tax at a rate of 30% and gives double tax relief by the credit method.

Below is an extract from Ying's statement of profit or loss for the year.

	$'000
Gross profit	2,130
Tax	(450)
Net profit for the year	900

Underlying tax is $40,000.

How much tax is payable by Yang in Country B in respect of the dividend received from Ying?

$ ☐

20.9 Company P has input tax for the quarter of $57,000. 50% of this is attributable to exempt outputs and the other 50% is attributable to zero-rated outputs.

How much input tax can it reclaim?

$ [   ]

20.10 A company has made sales in a period of $264,500, including sales tax. Its purchases excluding sales tax were $170,000, including zero rated items of $20,000.

If the rate of sales tax is 15%, how much is payable to the tax authorities?

- ☐ $12,000
- ☐ $14,935
- ☐ $17,175
- ☐ $20,110

21 Working capital and the operating cycle

21.1 An entity's working capital financing policy is to finance working capital using short-term financing to fund all the fluctuating current assets as well as some of the permanent part of the current assets.

The above policy is an example of:

- ☐ An aggressive policy
- ☐ A conservative policy
- ☐ A short-term policy
- ☐ A moderate policy

21.2 **Which of the following is NOT a symptom of overtrading?**

- ☐ Increasing levels of inventory
- ☐ Increasing levels of trade receivables
- ☐ Increasing levels of current liabilities
- ☐ Increasing levels of long term borrowings

21.3 The following information relates to Company X:

Trade receivable collection period	54 days
Raw material inventory turnover period	46 days
Work in progress inventory turnover period	32 days
Trade payables payment period	67 days
Finished goods inventory turnover period	43 days

What is the length of the working capital cycle?

- ☐ 134 days
- ☐ 156 days
- ☐ 108 days
- ☐ 150 days

21.4 **Which of the following would NOT be associated with a company that is overtrading?**

- ☐ A dramatic reduction in sales revenue
- ☐ A rapid increase in the outstanding overdraft amount
- ☐ A rapid increase in the volume of inventory
- ☐ A rapid increase in sales revenue

21.5 **Which THREE of the following statements are true with regards over-capitalisation?**

☐ Shareholders will not be happy as resources could be used elsewhere to generate a return
☐ The entity has invested too much in non-current assets
☐ The entity has invested too much in receivables, inventory and cash and holds few payables
☐ The entity has an excess of working capital
☐ The entity has invested too much in subsidiaries

21.6 The following information has been calculated for a business:

Trade receivable collection period 54 days
Trade payables payments period 67 days

If the working capital cycle is 102 days, what is the inventory turnover period?

☐ 19 days
☐ 115 days
☐ 89 days
☐ 13 days

21.7 An extract from a company's trial balance at the end of its financial year is given below.

	$'000
Sales revenue (85% on credit)	2,600
Cost of sales	1,800
Purchases (90% on credit)	1,650
Inventory of finished goods	220
Trade receivables	350
Trade payables	260

Calculate the following working capital ratios.

Show your answer to 1 decimal point.

Inventory days [＿＿＿＿]
Trade receivables days [＿＿＿＿]

21.8 **A company's working capital cycle can be calculated as:**

☐ Inventory days plus accounts receivable days less accounts payable days
☐ Accounts receivable days plus accounts payable days less inventory days
☐ Inventory days plus accounts payable days less accounts receivable days
☐ Accounts payable days plus accounts receivable days plus inventory days

21.9 RS reviews the financial performance of potential customers before setting a credit limit. The summarised financial statements for PQ, a potential major customer operating in the retail industry, are shown below.

Summary Statement of Financial Position for PQ at year end

	20X1	20X0
	$'000	$'000
Non-current assets	6,400	5,600
Inventories	1,200	1,120
Trade receivables	800	840
Cash	200	40
Trade payables	(1,120)	(1,160)
Non-current liabilities	(3,600)	(3,200)
Net assets	3,880	3,240
Share capital	2,400	2,400
Retained earnings	1,480	840
	3,880	3,240

Summary Statement of Profit or Loss for PQ for the years

	20X1	20X0
	$'000	$'000
Sales	12,000	10,000
Cost of sales	6,400	5,200
Profit before interest and tax	2,400	1,800

Calculate the following ratios, to the nearest 0.1 days, for PQ for 20X1.

Receivables days	
Payables days	

21.10 **Which one of the following transactions will affect the overall amount of working capital?**

- ☐ Receipt of the full amount of cash from a trade receivable
- ☐ Payment of an account payable
- ☐ Sale of a non-current asset on credit at its carrying amount
- ☐ Purchase of inventory on credit

22 Cash flow forecasts

22.1 EX is preparing its cash forecast for the next three months.

Which ONE of the following items should be left out of its calculations?

- ☐ Expected gain on the disposal of a piece of land
- ☐ Tax payment due, that relates to last year's profits
- ☐ Rental payment on a leased vehicle
- ☐ Receipt of a new bank loan raised for the purpose of purchasing new machinery

22.2 AB is preparing its cash budget for next year. The accounts receivable at the beginning of next year are expected to be $460,000. The budgeted sales are $5,400,000 and will occur evenly throughout the year. 80% of the budgeted sales will be on credit and the remainder will be cash sales. Credit customers pay in the month following sale.

What are the budgeted cash receipts from customers next year?

- ☐ $5,040,000
- ☐ $5,410,000
- ☐ $5,500,000
- ☐ $4,420,000

22.3 An entity is preparing its cash forecast for the next six months.

Which of the following items should be excluded from the calculations?

- ☐ Payments of last year's tax assessments
- ☐ Monthly payments due on the building rental
- ☐ Receipt of a bank loan negotiated for the purchase of a new office building
- ☐ An expected gain on the disposal of an old factory site

22.4 Claw is preparing its cash flow forecast for the next quarter.

Which of the following items should be excluded from the cash flow forecast?

☐   The receipt of a bank loan that has been raised for the purpose of investment in a new rolling mill

☐   Depreciation of the new rolling mill

☐   A tax payment that is due to be made which relates to profits earned in a previous accounting period

☐   Disposal proceeds from the sale of the old rolling mill

22.5 The cash flow forecast prepared by Heavy Metal Co suggests that the overdraft limit will be exceeded during the second month of the forecast period due to the timing of the asset purchase.

However, by the end of the quarter the overdraft should be back to a level similar to that at the start of the period.

Which ONE of the following courses of action would you recommend to overcome this problem?

☐   Acquire the asset using a finance lease rather than by outright purchase

☐   Seek help from an external company that can provide long term investment

☐   Make a share issue to raise the additional funds

☐   Negotiate with the bank for a short-term loan to cover the deficit

---

22.6 DY's trade receivables balance at 1 April 20X6 was $22,000. DY's income statement showed revenue from credit sales of $290,510 during the year ended 31 March 20X7.

DY's trade receivables at 31 March 20X7 were 49 days.

Assume DY's sales occur evenly throughout the year and that all balances outstanding at 1 April 20X6 have been received.

Also, it should be assumed all sales are on credit there were no bad debts and no trade discount was given.

How much cash did DY receive from its customers during the year to 31 March 20X7?

☐ $268,510

☐ $273,510

☐ $312,510

☐ $351,510

22.7 A trainee management account had prepared part of a company's budget for the next 6 months.

	Balances at 31 March (actual) $000	Balances at 30 September (budgeted) $000
Raw materials trade payables	58	47
Closing inventory of raw materials	39	51

The budget for the cost of raw materials used in the six month period to 30 September is $372,000.

Calculate the cash required to pay the raw materials trade payables for the period ended 30 September.

Give your answer to the nearest $000.

$'000

☐

22.8 Moon a printing business, has annual sales of $1.1 million and a gross profit margin of 50%. It is currently experiencing short-term cash flow difficulties, and intends to delay its payments to trade suppliers by one month.

To the nearest $, calculate the amount by which the cash balance will benefit in the short-term from this change in policy, assuming sales are spread evenly over the year, and inventory levels remain constant throughout.

The amount by which the cash balance will benefit in the short-term from this change in policy is:

$ [   ]

22.9 Fenton Co's projected revenue for 20X1 is $50,000.

It is forecast that 25% of sales will occur in January and the remaining sales will be earned equally among the remaining eleven months. All sales are on credit.

Customers' accounts are settled 55% in the month of sale and 40% in the following month. 5% of sales are written off as irrecoverable debts after two months.

Calculate the estimated receipts for March.

$ [   ]

22.10 Toaster Co is a trading company that does not hold any inventory.

Each month the following relationships hold:

Gross profit   25% of sales
Closing trade payables 15% of cost of sales

Sales are expected to be $40,000 in April and $48,000 in May.

How much will Toaster Co pay to its suppliers in May?

(Enter to nearest $)

$ [   ]

---

23 Cash management

23.1 **Which one of the following statements about an overdraft facility is correct?**

☐ An overdraft is a permanent loan
☐ Assets are always required as security
☐ Interest is paid on the full facility
☐ Compared with other types of loan it is quick and easy to set up

---

23.2 **Which of the following is NOT a feature of an agreed overdraft facility?**

☐ The borrower may draw funds, up to the agreed overdraft limit, as and when required

☐ Interest is payable on the total amount of the agreed overdraft limit rather than on the amount borrowed

☐ There is no fixed repayment date for the amount borrowed

☐ The borrowing is repayable on demand

23.3 Which of the following is NOT a form of short-term investment?

- ☐ Treasury bills
- ☐ Trade receivable factoring
- ☐ Local authority bonds
- ☐ Bank deposits

23.4 Which of the following is NOT a form of short-term finance?

- ☐ Bank overdraft
- ☐ Credit from trade payables
- ☐ Bank loans less than 6 months
- ☐ Treasury bills

23.5 Which of the following is an advantage for an entity of securing an overdraft rather than a short-term fixed-interest loan?

- ☐ Budgeting for cash is easier with an overdraft
- ☐ An overdraft is technically repayable on demand
- ☐ The entity's cash flows are more certain with the overdraft
- ☐ The terms of an overdraft are more easily changed to accommodate different needs within the entity

23.6 'A document issued by a bank on behalf of a customer authorising a person to draw money to a specified amount from its branches or correspondents, usually in another country, when the conditions set out in the document have been met.'

What does the above statement define?

- ☐ Bill of exchange
- ☐ Export guarantee
- ☐ Banker's draft
- ☐ Letter of credit

23.7 KEN is awaiting the go-ahead to start its new building programme. This is likely to take place within the next 90 days, but the precise start date and timing of the cash flows are still uncertain. The company has $150,000 available in cash in anticipation of the investment.

Which of the following is the LEAST appropriate use of the funds in the interim period?

- ☐ Investment in equities
- ☐ Treasury bills
- ☐ Bank deposits
- ☐ Local authority deposits

23.8 Which one of the following MOST appropriately describes forfaiting?

- ☐ It is a method of providing medium-term export finance
- ☐ It provides long-term finance to importers
- ☐ It provides equity finance for the redemption of shares
- ☐ It is the surrender of a share because of the failure to make a payment on a partly-paid share

23.9 Which of the following statements about certificates of deposit is FALSE?

- ☐ Certificates of deposit are negotiable instruments issued by banks
- ☐ Certificates of deposit will typically have maturity periods of between three and five years
- ☐ Certificates of deposit are non-negotiable
- ☐ Certificates of deposit are issued in bearer form

23.10 Which of the following statements best describes a documentary credit?

☐ A negotiable instrument, drawn by one party on another, who by signing the document acknowledges the debt, which may be payable immediately or at some future date

☐ A document issued by a bank on behalf of a customer authorising a person to draw money to a specified amount from its branches or correspondents, usually in another country, when the conditions set out in the document have been met

☐ A series of promissory notes, guaranteed by a highly rated international bank, and purchased at a discount to face value by an exporter's bank

☐ A form of export finance where the debt is sold to a factor, at a discount, in return for prompt cash

24 Receivables and payables

24.1 Which of the following services is LEAST LIKELY to be offered by a factoring company?

☐ Provision of finance by advancing, say 80% of invoice value immediately, and the remainder on settlement of the debt by the customer

☐ Taking over responsibility for administration of the client's sales ledger

☐ Deciding what credit limits customers should be given

☐ Non-recourse finance, i.e. taking over responsibility for irrecoverable debts

24.2 Which one of the following is NOT a stage in the credit cycle?

☐ Negotiation of the price of the goods
☐ Receipt of the customer order
☐ Checking the credit limit
☐ Goods despatched with delivery note

24.3 Which of the following sentences best describes invoice discounting?

☐ Reducing or discounting the amount owed by a customer in order to ensure payment

☐ Writing off a debt because the customer is not expected to pay

☐ Selling invoices to a finance company that then collects the cash from the customer

☐ Selling invoices to a finance company for less than their face value while continuing to collect the cash from the customer

24.4 Which of the following would NEVER be considered a feature of factoring?

☐ The factoring company charges a fee for its services

☐ Interest is charged on the amount advanced to the client from the date of the advance until the debt is settled by the client's customer

☐ The factoring company advances a percentage of the invoice value immediately, with the remainder being paid when the client's customer settles the debt

☐ The borrowing is repayable over a number of years

24.5 If an entity regularly fails to pay its suppliers by the normal due dates, it may lead to a number of problems.

Which TWO of the following problems could result from exceeding suppliers' trade credit terms?

☐   Having insufficient cash to pay debts as they fall due
☐   Difficulty in obtaining credit from new suppliers
☐   Reduction in credit rating
☐   Exceeding the bank's overdraft limit

24.6 DEN is considering whether to factor its sales ledger. It has been offered a 'without recourse' package by the factor at a cost of 2% sales, plus an administration fee of $5,000 per year. Annual sales are currently $1m, with bad debts of 1%.

What is the annual cost of the package to DEN likely to be?

☐ $5,000
☐ $20,000
☐ $24,800
☐ $25,000

24.7 GOR is considering changing its credit policy. It currently allows customers 90 days credit, but suffers irrecoverable debts amounting to 3% of its annual sales of $2m. It is proposing to reduce the credit period to 30 days, which should cause the irrecoverable debts to fall to 1% of turnover. However, it expects that this will result in a reduction in sales of 20%. This reduction will also be reflected in the level of purchases and inventory holding.

If GOR's current figures are:

Inventories (raw materials and finished goods)	$500,000
Annual purchases	$360,000
Payables	$30,000
Cost of capital	10%

What will be the effect of this on the annual financing cost?

☐   Saving of $46,000
☐   Increase of $46,000
☐   Saving of $36,000
☐   Increase of $36,000

24.8 CD uses factoring to manage its trade receivables. The factor advances 80% of invoiced sales and charges interest at a rate of 12% per annum. CD has estimated sales revenue for next year of $2,190,000. The average time for the factor to receive payment from customers is 50 days.

What will the estimated interest charge payable to the factor for next year be?

☐ $28,800
☐ $262,800
☐ $210,240
☐ $36,000

24.9 AB entity has trade payables at the year-end of $23,000. AB's cost of sales for the year are $103,628, opening inventory was $8,000 and closing inventory at the year end is $12,000. All purchases are on credit.

Calculate the trade payable days ratio:

☐☐☐ days

24.10 NC enjoys a 60 day credit period from all of its suppliers and has the following trade payables report:

Account number	Supplier name	Balance $	Up to 30 days $	31 -60 days $	61-90 days $	Over 90 days $
100378	X Co	250	50	200	-	-
100507	Y Co	1,000	-	-	-	1,000
103249	Z Co	750	150	300	300	-
Total		2,000	200	500	300	1,000
Percentage		100%	10%	25%	15%	50%

Which TWO of the following statements are NOT true?

- ☐ The debt to Y Co is over 90 days old and there may be a loss of goodwill
- ☐ X Co will be dissatisfied with what NC owe them
- ☐ Overall NC are very good at paying suppliers within due dates
- ☐ The amount owed to Z Co after the allowable credit period is $300
- ☐ The table is called an aged analysis table

25 Managing inventory

25.1 **Which one of the following is not considered to be a cost of holding inventory?**

- ☐ Loss of goodwill as a result of being unable to complete customer orders due to lack of inventory
- ☐ Insurance cost of inventory
- ☐ Storage cost of inventory
- ☐ Interest lost on cash invested in inventory

25.2 **Which FOUR of the following items SHOULD be included in arriving at the cost of the inventory of finished goods held by a manufacturing company, according to IAS 2 *Inventories*?**

- ☐ Carriage inwards on raw materials delivered to factory
- ☐ Carriage outwards on goods delivered to customers
- ☐ Factory supervisors' salaries
- ☐ Factory heating and lighting
- ☐ Cost of abnormally high idle time in the factory
- ☐ Import duties on raw materials

25.3 Shah's Shoes manufacture footwear. At the end of the year, 1,000 pairs of one line remain in inventory.

The costs involved in the manufacturing process are $3 in materials and $4 in labour per pair. The 1,000 pairs of shoes in inventory at the year end accounts for an estimated 2% of the factory's $100,000 annual overheads.

Selling costs are estimated at $2 per pair. The recommended retail price is $30 per pair, but Shah's normally sell them wholesale at 50% of this price. Sales have recently been flagging, compelling Shah's to offer a 30% trade discount on the wholesale price.

Calculate the value of inventory at the year end in accordance with IAS 2.

- ☐ $8,500
- ☐ $9,000
- ☐ $10,500
- ☐ $11,000

25.4   **Which THREE of the following describe situations where the net realisable value of inventory will be less than cost?**

☐   Increases in the selling price of goods sold
☐   Physical deterioration of inventory
☐   Increases in the cost of raw materials
☐   Errors in production or purchasing

25.5   An accountant is proposing to include overheads in closing inventory.

Which of the following statements correctly describes the treatment of overheads?

☐   Overheads may be included provided the absorption rates reflect normal activity levels

☐   Overheads must not be included

☐   Only under recoveries of overheads may be included

☐   The treatment is acceptable provided only production related overheads are included using a normal basis of activity to calculate the absorption rates

25.6   JD is a retailer of storage boxes. Annual demand is 39,000 units spread evenly throughout the year. Ordering costs are $100 per order and the cost of holding one storage box in inventory for one year is $1.60. It takes two weeks for an order to be delivered to JD's premises.

What is the economic order quantity (EOQ) for the storage boxes?

$$EOQ = \sqrt{\frac{2C_oD}{C_h}}$$

☐   1,746 units
☐   2,208 units
☐   2,793 units
☐   1,248 units

25.7   JD is a retailer of storage boxes. Annual demand is 39,000 units spread evenly throughout the year. Ordering costs are $100 per order and the cost of holding one storage box in inventory for one year is $1.60. It takes two weeks for an order to be delivered to JD's premises.

The re-order level that would ensure that JD never runs out of inventory of storage boxes is:

☐   1,560 units
☐   4,416 units
☐   3,492 units
☐   1,500 units

25.8 RS is a retailer of pet products. A dog basket that it sells has an annual demand of 15,000 units. Demand is spread evenly throughout the year.

RS pays its supplier $60 for each basket. Ordering costs are $150 per order and the annual cost of holding one basket in inventory is estimated to be $6.

What is the economic order quantity (EOQ) for the dog basket to the nearest unit?

$$EOQ = \sqrt{\frac{2C_o D}{C_h}}$$

- ☐ 612 units
- ☐ 173 units
- ☐ 866 units
- ☐ 1,025 units

25.9 IT has 300 items of product ABC2 in inventory at 31 March 20X9. The items were found to be damaged by a water leak. The items can be repaired and repackaged for a cost of $1.50 per item. Once repackaged, the items can be sold at the normal price of $3.50 each.

The original cost of the items was $2.20 each. The replacement cost at 31 March 20X9 is $2.75 each.

What value should IT put on the inventory of ABC2 in its statement of financial position at 31 March 20X9?

- ☐ $600
- ☐ $660
- ☐ $810
- ☐ $825

25.10 **Which of the following is NOT true regarding IAS 2 *Inventories*?**

- ☐ Fixed production overheads must be allocated to items of inventory on the basis of the normal level of production

- ☐ Plant lying idle will lead to a higher fixed overhead allocation to each unit

- ☐ An abnormally high level of production will lead to a lower allocation of fixed production overhead to each unit

- ☐ Unallocated overheads must be recognised as an expense in the period in which they are incurred

26 Mixed Bank 1

26.1 **Which of the following is NOT an advantage of global harmonisation of accounting standards?**

- ☐ Priority given to different user groups in different countries
- ☐ Easier transfer of accounting staff across national borders
- ☐ Ability to comply with the requirements of overseas stock exchanges
- ☐ Better access to foreign investor funds

26.2 **Which TWO of the following characterise faithful representation in the IASB's *Conceptual framework for financial reporting*?**

- ☐ Use of information that has the ability to influence decisions
- ☐ Information that is free from error
- ☐ Information that is complete

26.3 **Which TWO of the following non-current assets would normally require depreciation?**

☐ Freehold land
☐ Freehold buildings
☐ Freehold investment property
☐ Plant and machinery

26.4 AB is an entity that manufactures motor vehicles. One division has historically made vintage cars however the market for such cars has been in decline over the past few years and AB has seen this division make significant losses. As such the directors decided to close the division on 30 June 20X4 and at that point all of the division's assets were classified as held for sale.

You have the following information:

	$'000
Carrying amount at 1 January 20X4	250
Fair value at 30 June 20X4	232
Value in use at 30 June 20X4	231
Anticipated costs to sell at 30 June 20X4	7

The depreciation for the year ended 31 December 20X4 had the assets not been classified as held for sale would have been $30,000.

The asset had not been sold at the year end of 31 December 20X4.

Calculate the value at which the division's assets should be shown in the statement of financial position.

$ [   ]

26.5 ASD operates a defined benefit pension plan. At 1 January 20X2 the present value of the pension plan liabilities was $5,500,000.

The actuary estimates that the service cost for the year ended 31 December 20X2 is $1,020,000 and the relevant discount rate was 4% for the year ended 31 December 20X2. The pension plan paid $280,000 to retired members and ASD paid $820,000 in contributions to the pension plan for the year ended 31 December 20X2.

At 31 December 20X2 the present value of the pension plan liabilities is $6,400,000.

What is the re-measurement gain or loss on the pension plan liabilities at 31 December 20X2?

☐ Gain $60,000
☐ Loss $60,000
☐ Gain $880,000
☐ Loss $880,000

26.6 PA acquired 75% of the equity shares of SD for $280,800. The remaining 25% was valued at $64,800.

The net assets of SD at acquisition were $306,000.

Assuming that the non-controlling interest is valued using the fair value method, which of the following is the correct value that should be included for goodwill in the consolidated statement of financial position?

☐ $51,300
☐ $39,600
☐ $116,100
☐ $(46,800)

26.7 What is 'hypothecation'?

☐ Process of earmarking tax revenues for specific types of expenditure
☐ Estimation of tax revenue made by the tax authorities for budget purposes
☐ Refund made by tax authorities for tax paid in other countries
☐ Payment of taxes due to tax authorities, net of tax refunds due from tax authorities

26.8 Which ONE of the following would be considered to be an example of an indirect tax?

☐ An entity assessed for corporate income tax on its profit
☐ An individual purchases goods in a shop, the price includes VAT
☐ An employee has tax deducted from salary through the PAYE system
☐ An individual pays capital gains tax on a gain arising on the disposal of an investment

26.9 HMP has decided to adopt a moderate working capital policy. It has fluctuating current assets of $1m, permanent current assets of $5m, and non-current assets of $9m.

Which of the following mixes of finance is the company MOST LIKELY to choose?

☐ Short-term financing of $1m; permanent financing of $14m
☐ Short-term financing of $0.5m; permanent financing of $14.5m
☐ Short-term financing of $2m; permanent financing of $13m
☐ Short-term financing of $4m; permanent financing of $11m

26.10 Z Co is considering selling its receivables to a debt factor.

The debt factor will pay 90% of the value of invoices finally paid with the balance kept as their service charge. Z Co normally gets 40% of the amount invoiced within 30 days. 80% of the remaining balance is usually received after 60 days with the remaining 20% written off as irrecoverable.

The debt factor tends to suffer irrecoverable debts amounting to $10 in every $100 invoiced.

If Z Co sells its debts to the debt factor, by how much will cash flow change for every $100 factored?

☐ $2 increase
☐ $1 increase
☐ $7 decrease
☐ $8 decrease

27 Mixed Bank 2

27.1 Which body issues International Financial Reporting Standards?

☐ The IFRS Advisory Council
☐ The IFRS Foundation
☐ The International Accounting Standards Board
☐ The IFRS Interpretations Committee

27.2 Which THREE of the following are NOT an underlying assumption from the IASB's *Conceptual Framework for Financial Reporting*?

☐ Accruals
☐ Going concern
☐ Faithful representation
☐ Relevance

27.3 Which of the following would NOT be classed as a non-current asset?

- ☐ Freehold property, occupied by the entity, held for its investment potential
- ☐ Freehold property, not occupied by the entity, held for its investment potential
- ☐ Shares in another company held as a short-term store of spare cash
- ☐ A 'limited edition' delivery van used in the entity's operations
- ☐ All the statements listed

27.4 On 1 September 20X7, the directors of EK decided to sell EK's retailing division and concentrate activities entirely on its manufacturing division.

The retailing division was available for immediate sale, but EK had not succeeded in disposing of the operation by 31 October 20X7. EK identified a potential buyer for the retailing division, but negotiations were at an early stage. The directors of EK are certain that the sale will be completed by 31 August 20X8.

Where should the assets of the retailing division be shown in the statement of financial position as at 31 October 20X7?

- ☐ Under non-current assets
- ☐ Under current assets
- ☐ They should not be included in the statement of financial position
- ☐ Included within receivables

27.5 An entity has a defined benefit pension plan and the actuary has provided the following values:

	At December 20X1 $'000	At 1 January 20X1 $'000
Fair value of pension plan assets	1,314	1,080

Other information in respect of the year ended 31 December 20X1 is as follows:

	$'000
Contributions paid	450
Benefits paid	342
Current service cost	540
Interest income on plan assets	86

What is the re-measurement gain or loss on the pension plan assets?

- ☐ Gain $40,000
- ☐ Loss $40,000
- ☐ Gain $580,000
- ☐ Loss $580,000

27.6 Which TWO of the following conditions need to be satisfied for a parent entity to be exempt from preparing consolidated financial statements according to IFRS 10 *Consolidated Financial Statements*?

- ☐ Parent entity only has one subsidiary
- ☐ Parent entity is itself partially owned but has consent from the non-controlling interest
- ☐ Parent is itself a wholly owned subsidiary
- ☐ Parent entity holds less than 75% interest in the subsidiary
- ☐ Subsidiary's activities are dissimilar to that of its parent

27.7 An entity sells furniture and adds a sales tax to the selling price of all products sold. A customer purchasing furniture from the entity has to pay the cost of the furniture plus the sales tax. The customer therefore bears the cost of the sales tax.

What type of incidence is this referred to as?

☐ Formal incidence
☐ Indirect incidence
☐ Effective incidence
☐ Direct incidence

27.8 **Which of the following is an indirect tax?**

☐ Withholding tax
☐ Employee tax
☐ Sales tax
☐ Corporate income tax

27.9 A company has annual sales revenues of $48 million. The company earns a constant gross margin of 40% on sales. All sales and purchases are on credit and are evenly distributed over the year.

The following are maintained at a constant level throughout the year:

Inventory $8 million
Trade receivables $10 million
Trade payables $5 million

What is the company's cash operating cycle to the nearest day?

☐ 99 days
☐ 114 days
☐ 89 days
☐ 73 days

27.10 **Which ONE of the following statements best describes the invoice discounting service offered by a factoring company?**

☐ The factoring company takes over the administration of the client's invoicing system

☐ The factoring company enforces the correct administration of the client's system of offering cash discounts, and ensures that discounts are disallowed in line with policy

☐ The factoring company advances finance to the client against the debts which the factor has purchased, up to 80% of the value of the debts

☐ The factoring company purchases a selection of invoices, at a discount, thus providing the client with a source of short-term finance

28 Mixed Bank 3

28.1 **Which recommendation of the Sarbanes-Oxley Act addresses the problem of over-familiarity of the audit firm with the client?**

☐ Rotation of lead audit partner every year
☐ Rotation of lead audit partner every five years
☐ Rotation of audit firms every three years
☐ Rotation of audit firms every seven years
☐ Audit partner not to become chair of the internal audit committee

28.2 Which TWO of the following options are benefits which accrue from having a conceptual framework such as the IASB's *Conceptual Framework for Financial Reporting*?

☐   The information needs of all user groups will be better served
☐   Accounting standards will develop in a more coherent fashion
☐   Different accounting presentation of transactions not currently covered by IAS/IFRS should reduce
☐   The task of developing and implementing standards will become easier

28.3 Which of the following would not be classified as an investment property according to IAS 40 *Investment property*?

☐   Land being held for capital appreciation
☐   A building rented out to a third party
☐   Property that is being constructed for future use as an investment property
☐   Property being constructed on behalf of third parties

28.4 On 1 March 20X5, the directors of YS decided to sell YS's manufacturing division. The division was available for immediate sale, but YS had not succeeded in disposing of the operation by 31 August 20X5 (the reporting date). YS identified a potential buyer for the division, but negotiations were ongoing, the directors are however certain that the sale will be completed within the next three months.

The manufacturing division's carrying amount at 1 March 20X5 was $443,000 and it had a fair value of $423,000.

YS's directors have estimated that YS will incur consultancy and legal fees for the disposal of $25,000.

Calculate the value of the impairment loss suffered by YS on classification of the manufacturing division as held for sale.

$ ☐

28.5 QWS operates a defined benefit pension plan for its employees; At 1 July 20X2 the fair value of the pension plan assets was $1,200,000 and the present value of the pension plan liabilities was $1,400,000; The yield on high quality corporate bonds was 7%.

The actuary estimates that the current service cost for the year ended 30 June 20X3 is $300,000; QWS made contributions into the pension plan of $400,000 in the year.

The net expense that will be included in QWS's profit and loss for the year ended 30 June 20X3 is:

$ ☐

28.6 CD acquired 60% of the share capital of MB on 1 April 20X3 for $42 million when its retained earnings were $7 million.

The equity sections of the statement of financial position of both companies at 31 March 20X4 are:

	CD	MB
	$m	$m
Share capital - $1 shares	86	22
Retained earnings	26	12
	112	34

Goodwill of $28 million arose on acquisition. An impairment loss of $4 million had arisen at the year ending 31 March 20X4. It is the group policy to value non-controlling interest at the proportionate share of the net assets at acquisition.

What figure for consolidated retained earnings should appear in the consolidated statement of financial position at 31 March 20X4?

- ☐ $27 million
- ☐ $29.2 million
- ☐ $25 million
- ☐ $26.6 million

28.7 **The term 'tax gap' describes the difference between:**

- ☐ When a tax payment is due and the date it is actually paid
- ☐ The tax due calculated by the entity and the tax demanded by the tax authority
- ☐ The amount of tax due to be paid and the amount actually collected
- ☐ The date when the entity was notified by the tax authority of the tax due and the date the tax should be paid

28.8 **Which of the following "persons" bears the cost of a sales tax?**

- ☐ The supplier of raw materials
- ☐ The end consumer
- ☐ The retailer
- ☐ The wholesaler

28.9 A company has annual sales revenues of $30 million and the following working capital periods:

Inventory conversion period	2.5 months
Accounts receivable collection period	2.0 months
Accounts payable equates to	$2.625 million

Production costs represent 70% of sales revenue.

Calculate the total amount held in working capital excluding cash and cash equivalents.

$☐ million

28.10 **Which THREE of the following services does a factor most commonly offer?**

- ☐ Administration of the client's payables ledger department
- ☐ Provision of finance against the client's outstanding receivables
- ☐ Protection against irrecoverable debts
- ☐ Administration of the client's invoicing and debt collection
- ☐ Provision of credit rating information for prospective customers

29 Mixed Bank 4

29.1 You are the audit partner in charge of the audit of PT Co. PT has draft revenue of $100m and draft profit of $10m.

The following matter has been brought to your attention.

A large customer of PT has gone bankrupt. There are receivables balances in the draft accounts of PT that total $2m. The recoverability of these balances is highly doubtful, but PT has refused to make an allowance against them.

You conclude that the issue is not fundamental to the accounts.

What type of audit opinion should you issue in this circumstance?

☐   Unmodified opinion

☐   Modified - qualified opinion (due to insufficient appropriate audit evidence)

☐   Modified - qualified opinion (due to material misstatement)

☐   Modified - adverse opinion

29.2   The IASB's *Conceptual Framework for Financial Reporting* requires information to be faithfully represented.

Which of the following is an aspect of faithful representation as defined in the IASB's Conceptual Framework?

☐   Classification

☐   Consistency

☐   Neutrality

☐   Predictive value

29.3   **Which TWO of the following journals are acceptable to record the transfer of deferred income to the statement of profit or loss and other comprehensive income under IAS 20 *Government grants*?**

☐   Dr The related expense, Cr Deferred income

☐   Dr Deferred income, Cr Other income

☐   Dr Deferred income, Cr The related expense

☐   Dr Other income, Cr Deferred income

29.4   SA has two divisions, division A and division B. On 31 March 20X3, SA's management board agreed to dispose of its loss-making division B and it was classified as "held for sale" in accordance with IFRS 5 *Noncurrent assets held for sale and discontinued operations*.

Below is an extract from the notes to the financial statements for the discontinuing operation:

	$'000
Revenue	185
Cost of Sales	(230)
Gross loss	(45)
Administrative expenses (before depreciation)	(30)
Depreciation on assets classified as held for sale	
Distribution costs	(125)
Closure costs	(78)
Tax refund	40
Loss on adjustment in asset's value to fair value	

Additional information:

(i)   Division B has the following assets at 31 March 20X3:

	Cost	Accumulated depreciation at 1 April 20X2
	$'000	$'000
Factory	460	23
Plant and equipment	180	140

(ii)   Plant and equipment depreciation is provided at 20% per year on the reducing balance basis. Buildings are depreciated at 2.5% per year on a straight line basis.

(iii)   The fair value of division B's net assets at 31 March 20X3 was $431,000.

Calculate, to the nearest $'000, the value of the "depreciation on assets classified as held for sale" and the "loss on adjustment in asset's value to fair value".

$'000

Depreciation on assets classified as held for sale: ☐

Loss on adjustment in asset's value to fair value: ☐

29.5 **Which TWO of the following items in respect of a defined benefit pension plan should be recognised in the statement of profit or loss?**

☐ Current service cost
☐ Re-measurement of gain on plan liabilities
☐ Unwinding of discount on plan liabilities
☐ Contributions paid into scheme

29.6 A subsidiary transfers $15,000 to its parent entity on 31 March, the last day of its financial year. The parent did not receive the transfer until 3 April.

Complete the following journal entry for the adjustment required to the consolidated statement of financial position.

Write the name of the other account and identify whether the entries should be a debit or a credit.

Cash and cash equivalents	$15,000	
	$15,000	

29.7 BM has a taxable profit of $30,000 and receives a tax assessment of $3,000. BV has a taxable profit of $60,000 and receives a tax assessment of $7,500.

BM and BV are resident in the same tax jurisdiction.

Which tax rate structure operates in this jurisdiction?

☐ A progressive tax
☐ A regressive task
☐ A direct tax
☐ A proportional tax

29.8 **When an entity is resident for tax purposes in more than one country, the OCED model tax convention states that an entity will be deemed to be resident only in its:**

☐ Place of permanent establishment
☐ Place of effective management
☐ Place of incorporation
☐ Place of main business activity

29.9 BC had trade receivables of $242,000 at the start of the year. BC forecasts that the sales revenue for the year will be $1,500,000. All sales are on credit.

Trade receivable days at the end of the year are expected to be 60 days based on a 365 day year.

What are the expected receipts from customers during the year ?

☐ $1,495,425
☐ $1,742,000
☐ $ 1,253,425
☐ $ 1,504,575

29.10 A company is offering its customers the choice of a cash discount of 3% for payment within 15 days of the invoice date or paying in full within 45 days.

What is the effective annual interest rate of the cash discount?

- ☐ 43.3%
- ☐ 12.5%
- ☐ 44.9%
- ☐ 24.7%

30 Mixed Bank 5

30.1 The auditor of X Co expresses his opinion of the financial statements in terms of their truth and fairness.

Why does explicit reference to the term 'true and fair' arise?

- ☐ It is a requirement of CIMA

- ☐ Its use is self-evident as all audited financial statements must be prepared with the intention of giving a true and fair view

- ☐ Use of the term is established best practice but is not prescribed by legislation or regulation

- ☐ ISA 700 *Forming an opinion and reporting on financial statements* prescribes its use

30.2 Burrows Co is a soft drinks manufacturer.

Which of the following items must be disclosed on the face of the statement of profit or loss?

All items are material.

- ☐ Loss on closure of bottling division
- ☐ Irrecoverable debt as a result of bankruptcy of a major customer
- ☐ Profit on a sale of outdated mixing machinery
- ☐ Fall in value of head office building due to recession

30.3 Westland had the following loans in place throughout 20X8:

| 10% bank loan | $100 million |
| 8% bank loan | $80 million |

On 1 January 20X8 it began construction of a power generation plant. Funds drawn down were $40 million on 1 January 20X8 and a further $30 million on 1 July 20X8. The construction was still ongoing at the year end date of 31 December 20X8.

Calculate the amount of borrowing costs that can be capitalised for the year. (Calculate your interest rate to the nearest whole number).

- ☐ $4.95 million
- ☐ $5.5 million
- ☐ $4.4 million
- ☐ $3.15 million

30.4 IAS 21 standardises the treatment of transactions denominated in foreign currency. The accounting methods in use depend upon whether the item(s) concerned are monetary or non-monetary items.

Which THREE of the following are 'monetary items' as far as IAS 21 is concerned?

☐ Long-term bank deposits
☐ Amounts payable to a foreign leasing company
☐ An acquisition of a new machine from a foreign supplier
☐ The balance due from an overseas company in relation to export sales

---

30.5 The following balances appear in the statement of financial position of Lea Co.

	Year ending 31 March	
	20X5	20X4
	$'000	$'000
Non-current assets at cost	1,250	1,096
Revaluation surplus	240	140

During the year ended 31 March 20X5 non-current assets with a cost of $150,000 were disposed of.

Calculate the amount that would appear in the statement of cash flows for the purchase of non-current assets.

$ _____

30.6 OP owns 90% of ST. The retained earnings of ST at acquisition were $560,000.

During the current accounting period OP sold an item of plant to ST for $200,000. This plant had a carrying amount of $120,000 and a remaining useful life of 4 years.

The retained earnings at the current year end for OP and ST respectively were $1,360,000 and $920,000.

Calculate the consolidated retained earnings for inclusion in the consolidated statement of financial position of the OP group at the end of the year.

$ _____

30.7 A Co has been trading for a number of years and is resident for tax purposes in Country X.

The tax written down value of A Co's property, plant and equipment was $40,000 at 31 March 20X8. A Co did not purchase any property, plant and equipment between 1 April 20X8 and 31 March 20X9.

A Co's statement of profit or loss and other comprehensive income for the year ended 31 March 20X9 is as follows:

	$
Gross profit	270,000
Administrative expenses	(120,000)
Depreciation - property, plant and equipment	(12,000)
Distribution costs	(55,000)
Finance cost	(11,000)
Profit before tax	72,000

Administration expenses include entertaining of $15,000.

Relevant tax rules

Corporate profits

The rules for taxation of corporate profits are as follows:

- Accounting rules of recognition and measurement are followed for tax purposes
- All expenses other than depreciation, amortisation, entertaining, taxes paid to other public bodies and donations to political parties are tax deductible.
- The corporate tax on profits is at a rate of 25%

What is A Co's income tax due for the year ended 31 March 20X9?

☐ $8,750
☐ $13,750
☐ $15,500
☐ $22,250

30.8 A company has sales for the quarter of $400,000 net of sales tax. Half of its sales relate to goods which are exempt from VAT. It has input tax of $28,000, half of which is attributable to its exempt sales and therefore cannot be reclaimed. Sales tax is charged at a rate of 15%.

Calculate the balance owed to the tax authorities at the end of the quarter.

☐ $32,000
☐ $2,000
☐ $16,000
☐ $46,000

30.9 **Write in the box 'reducing' or 'increasing' to complete the sentence for the following three scenarios:**

The operational cash flows of a business could be improved directly by:

☐ receivables.

☐ inventory.

☐ the credit period from the company's trade suppliers.

30.10 **Which TWO of the following statements are correct?**

Replacement cost is calculated as the selling price of the inventory less any further costs to completion or costs of selling the inventory.	☐ TRUE	☐ FALSE
Average cost calculates a new weighted average cost calculated upon each delivery.	☐ TRUE	☐ FALSE
FIFO assumes that inventory is used in the order in which it is delivered.	☐ TRUE	☐ FALSE
Inventory may not be valued using a standard cost.	☐ TRUE	☐ FALSE
Net realisable value (NRV) values inventory at the current cost of acquisition.	☐ TRUE	☐ FALSE

31 Mixed Bank 6

31.1 **An unmodified opinion implies which of the following?**

☐ No errors or irregularities have been discovered by the auditor
☐ No errors or irregularities have been discovered during the accounting period
☐ The company has followed the provisions of IFRSs
☐ None of the above statements are correct

31.2 **Which of the following might appear as a separate item in the 'other comprehensive income' section of the statement of profit or loss and other comprehensive income?**

☐ A material irrecoverable debt arising in the year
☐ A share issue in the year
☐ An impairment loss on assets carried at depreciated historical cost
☐ An upward revaluation of the company's assets

31.3 **Which of the following statements is correct?**

☐   Negative goodwill should be shown in the statement of financial position as a deduction from positive goodwill

☐   IAS 38 allows purchased goodwill to be written off immediately against reserves as an alternative to capitalisation

☐   As a business grows, internally generated goodwill may be revalued upwards to reflect that growth

☐   Internally developed brands must not be capitalised

31.4   At the beginning of the year, company Y had an opening credit balance of $5,000 on its current tax account. Payments were made during the year of $7,500 and the tax due at the end of the year amounted to $25,000.

What is the charge to tax in the statement of profit or loss for the year?

☐ $25,000
☐ $27,500
☐ $30,000
☐ $32,500

31.5   Carrie Co is preparing its statement of cash flows.

Which of the following would need to be deducted from profit before tax in order to generate a figure for cash flows from operating activities?

☐   Write down for irrecoverable debts
☐   Write down for obsolete inventory
☐   Surplus on revaluation of property
☐   Profit on sale of a motor vehicle

31.6   The HC group acquired 30% of the equity share capital of AF on 1 April 20X0 paying $25,000.

At 1 April 20X0 the equity of AF comprised:

	$
$1 equity shares	50,000
Share premium	12,500
Retained earnings	10,000

AF made a profit for the year to 31 March 20X1 (prior to dividend distribution) of $6,500 and paid a dividend of $3,500 to its equity shareholders.

The value of HC's investment in AF for inclusion in HC's consolidated statement of financial position at 31 March 20X1 would be:

☐ $25,000
☐ $25,900
☐ $26,950
☐ $28,000

31.7 **Which ONE of the following is regarded as a direct tax?**

☐   Value added tax
☐   Capital gains tax
☐   Excise duties
☐   Property tax

31.8 Company J sells its goods all over the world. Its factory is in Spain, the sales are handled by a call-centre in India, the head office is in London and the registered office is in Switzerland.

All of the tax authorities involved use the OECD model tax convention as the basis of double taxation treaties between them.

Where will the tax authorities consider Company J's place of corporate residence to be?

☐ UK
☐ Switzerland
☐ India
☐ Spain

31.9 **Which of the following methods could NOT be used to reduce the risks of irrecoverable debts when trading overseas?**

☐ Export factoring
☐ Forfaiting
☐ Advances against collections
☐ Documentary credits

31.10 The Economic Order Quantity can be expressed as follows:

$$EOQ = \sqrt{\frac{2CoD}{Ch}}$$

What does Ch describe in this formula?

☐ The cost of holding one unit of inventory for one year
☐ The cost of placing one order
☐ The cost of a unit of inventory
☐ The customer demand for the item

32 Mixed Bank 7

32.1 **Which of the following would be a self-interest threat for an accountant in public practice?**

☐ Preparing accounts for an audit client
☐ Financial interest in a client's affairs
☐ Becoming too friendly with client staff
☐ Being threatened with litigation

32.2 B Co had the following transactions in non-current assets during the year to 31 October 20X9:

(i) A $16,000 write down in the value of some items of plant held at historical cost.
(ii) Upward revaluation of offices by $92,000.

What is the total amount that will be reported in other comprehensive income by B Co in relation to these transactions?

☐ $(16,000) loss
☐ $92,000 gain
☐ $76,000 gain
☐ $(16,000) loss and $92,000 gain separately disclosed

32.3 Which **TWO** of the following conditions would preclude any part of the development expenditure to which it relates from being capitalised?

☐   The development is incomplete

☐   The benefits flowing from the completed development are expected to be less than its cost

☐   Funds are unlikely to be available to complete the development

☐   The development is expected to give rise to more than one product

---

32.4 Which one of the following material items would be classified as a non-adjusting event in HL's financial statements for the year ended 31 December 20X8 according to IAS 10 *Events after the reporting period*?

HL's financial statements were approved for publication on 8 April 20X9.

☐   On 1 March 20X9, HL's auditors discovered that, due to an error during the count, the closing inventory had been undervalued by $250,000

☐   Lightning struck one of HL's production facilities on 31 January 20X9 and caused a serious fire. The fire destroyed half of the factory and its machinery. Output was severely reduced for six months

☐   One of HL's customers commenced court action against HL on 1 December 20X8. At 31 December 20X8, HL did not know whether the case would go against it or not. On 1 March 20X9, the court found against HL and awarded damages of $150,000 to the customer

☐   On 15 March 20X9, HL was advised by the liquidator of one of its customers that it was very unlikely to receive any payments for the balance of $300,000 that was outstanding at 31 December 20X8

32.5 The statement of cash flows is based on 'cash and cash equivalents' as defined by IAS 7 *'Statement of Cash Flows'*.

Which FOUR of the following items could be included in cash?

☐   Bank current account in domestic currency

☐   Short term deposit (three months notice period)

☐   Bank overdraft

☐   Petty cash float

☐   Bank current account in foreign currency

32.6 The HY group acquired 35% of the equity share capital of SX on 1 July 2010 paying $70,000. This shareholding enabled HY group to exercise significant influence over SX.

At 1 July 2010 the equity of SX comprised:

	$
$1 equity shares	100,000
Retained earnings	50,000

SX made a profit for the year ended 30 June 2011 (prior to dividend distribution) of $130,000 and paid a dividend of $80,000 to its equity shareholders.

Calculate the value of HY's investment in SX for inclusion in its consolidated statement of financial position at 30 June 2011.

$ ☐☐☐☐☐☐☐

32.7 Which **ONE** of the following gives the meaning of rollover relief?

☐   Trading losses can be carried forward to future years

☐   Inventory can be valued using current values instead of original cost

☐   Capital losses made in a period can be carried forward to future years

☐   Payment of tax on a capital gain can be delayed if the full proceeds from the sale of an asset are reinvested in a replacement asset

32.8 **A double taxation treaty:**

☐   Sets out which tax authority has jurisdiction
☐   Allows a company to be taxed twice on the same income
☐   Abolishes withholding tax
☐   Means companies do not have to pay foreign taxes

32.9 **Which of the following is NOT a method used for raising finance to fund export sales?**

☐   Bills of exchange
☐   Credit insurance
☐   Documentary credits
☐   Countertrade

32.10 Create Co requires 20,000 units of a certain component every year. The purchase price per unit is $40 and it costs $64 to place and receive delivery of an order irrespective of its size. Create Co's cost of capital is 10% per annum.

Create Co currently places orders for 800 units, although a discount scheme for larger orders exists which works as follows.

Minimum order quantity	Discount rate
1,000	1%
4,000	2%
8,000	3%

What size of order should Create Co place if its aim is to minimise costs?

☐   800 units
☐   1,000 units
☐   4,000 units
☐   8,000 units

33 Mixed Bank 8

33.1 **Which of the following is NOT one of the five fundamental principles of professional ethics in the CIMA Code of Ethics?**

☐   Integrity
☐   Objectivity
☐   Reliability
☐   Professional competence and due care
☐   Confidentiality

33.2 **Which TWO of the following are reasons why segment reporting in the financial statements is considered to be useful to readers of the accounts?**

☐   It can explain factors which have contributed to company results
☐   It is useful to separate out the performance of continuing and discontinued elements of the business
☐   It clearly shows the retained profit of different segments of the business
☐   Users can assess the future risks and rewards associated with the business

33.3 A cash generating unit comprises the following:

	$m
Building	20
Plant and equipment	10
Goodwill	5
Current assets	10
	45

Following a downturn in the market, an impairment review has been undertaken and the recoverable amount of the cash generating unit is estimated to be $25m.

What is the carrying amount of the building after adjusting for the impairment loss?

☐ $11 million
☐ $10 million
☐ $12.5 million
☐ $20 million

33.4 **Which THREE of the following events after the reporting period would normally be classified as *non-adjusting*, according to IAS 10 *Events after the reporting period*?**

☐ Opening new trading operations
☐ Sale of goods held at the year end for less than cost
☐ A customer is discovered to be insolvent
☐ Announcement of plan to discontinue an operation
☐ Expropriation (seizure) of major assets by government

33.5 Information concerning the non-current assets of Ealing Co is detailed in the table below.

During the year non-current assets which had cost $80,000 and which had a carrying amount of $30,000 were sold for $20,000.

The final figure for net cash flows from operating activities for the year was $300,000.

	Start of year	End of year
	$	$
Cost	180,000	240,000
Accumulated depreciation	(120,000)	(140,000)
Carrying amount	60,000	100,000

Non-current assets were not revalued during the year.

What was the increase in cash and cash equivalents for the year?

☐ $240,000
☐ $260,000
☐ $180,000
☐ $320,000

33.6 On 1 April 20X7 R acquired 40% of the share capital of H for $120,000 when the retained earnings of H were $80,000

During the year R sold goods to H for $30,000 including a profit margin of 25%. These goods were still in inventory at the year end.

At 31 March 20X8 the retained earnings of H were $140,000.

At what amount should R's interest in H be shown in the consolidated statement of financial position at 31 March 20X8?

☐ $173,000
☐ $144,000
☐ $141,000
☐ $105,000

33.7 P Co paid a dividend of $150,000 to its shareholders in the year ended 30 June 20X1. P Co is resident for tax purposes in Country X where the corporate rate of income tax is 25% and the personal rate of income tax is 30% on dividends received. Country X has an imputation system of tax.

How much tax is payable on the dividend received by the shareholders of P Co?

$ ▢

33.8 Tuton, a company resident in Country X, is a 100% owned subsidiary of Carmoon, a company resident in Country Y. At the year end, Tuton paid a dividend of $90,000 after deduction of withholding tax of $10,000, to Carmoon. Country Y charges corporate income tax at a rate of 40% and gives double tax relief by the credit method.

Below is an extract from Tuton's statement of profit or loss for the year.

	$'000
Gross profit	1,850
Tax	(240)
Net profit for the year	1,200

Underlying tax is $20,000

How much double tax relief is given to Carmoon in Country Y?

$ ▢

33.9 **Which of the following statements about bond rates are true?**

(I)   The coupon rate determines the amount of interest received annually.
(II)   The yield to maturity is the discount rate that should be used to discount the amounts received.

☐   Both statements are false
☐   Both statements are true
☐   Statement I is true and statement II is false
☐   Statement I is false and statement II is true

33.10 **Which of the following can the economic order quantity model be used to determine?**

(i)   The order quantity;
(i)   The buffer inventory;
(iii)   The re-order level.

☐   (i) and (iii)
☐   (i) and (ii)
☐   (ii) and (iii)
☐   (i) only

Answers to
objective test questions

1 Regulation and corporate governance

1.1   The correct answer is: The IFRS Interpretations Committee.

Guidance on application and interpretation of IFRSs is provided by the IFRS Interpretations Committee.

1.2   The correct answer is: IFRS Foundation Trustees.

The IFRS Foundation trustees are responsible for governance and fundraising and publish an annual report on the IASB's activities. The trustees also review annually the strategy of the IASB and its effectiveness.

1.3   The correct answer is: The IFRS Advisory Council.

1.4   The correct answer is: The system by which companies are directed and controlled.

All the other options are aspects of corporate governance but none provides a precise definition.

1.5   The correct answer is: The nomination committee should consist entirely of executive directors.

Corporate governance practice varies, but the UK Corporate Governance Code recommends that the majority of nomination committee members should be independent non-executive directors.

1.6   The correct answer is: The IFRS Interpretations Committee.

The IFRS Foundation is the parent entity of the IASB and the IFRS Advisory Committee advises the IASB on major standard-setting projects.

1.7   The correct answers are:

- Approving the annual budget of the IASB
- Reviewing the strategy of the IASB and its effectiveness
- Appointing members of the IASB, the IFRS Interpretations Committee and the IFRS Advisory Council

The IFRS Foundation Trustees are also responsible for establishing and amending the operating procedures, consultative arrangements and due process for the IASB, the Interpretations Committee and the Advisory Council

1.8   The correct answer is: One of the objectives of the IFRS Foundation is to bring about convergence of national accounting standards and IFRSs.

The IFRS Advisory Council is a forum for the IASB to consult with the outside world. The IASB produces IFRSs and is overseen by the IFRS Foundation.

1.9   The correct answers are:

- It focuses on objectives;
- It can be applied across different legal jurisdictions
- It can stress those areas where rules cannot easily be applied
- It puts the emphasis on investors making up their own minds.

Definite targets are characteristics of a rules-based approach, although many codes that are largely based on principles might include some targets.

1.10   The correct answers are:

- It emphasises measurable achievements by companies
- It can easily be applied in jurisdictions where the letter of the law is stressed.

A rules-based approach implies that companies must comply and do not have the option of explaining non-compliance. Rulebooks cannot normally cover all eventualities and hence a rules-based approach may have difficulty coping with situations that are not covered by the rulebook. A rules-based approach can be difficult to apply across different legal jurisdictions, because the rulebook will have to be compatible with variations in local law.

BPP
LEARNING MEDIA

2 External audit

2.1   The correct answer is: Form an opinion as to the truth and fairness of a set of financial statements.

An audit can at best give reasonable assurance that the financial statements are free from material misstatement. Auditors provide a professional opinion on the financial statements to the shareholders, they do not provide a certificate to directors and it would be impossible for them to state that the financial statements are 100% accurate.

2.2   The correct answer is: Identification of the accounting convention adopted by management in preparing the financial statements.

The auditor may choose to identify the accounting convention used in the preparation of the financial statements if he thinks that it would assist the user of the statements, but this is not a statutory or regulatory requirement.

2.3   The correct answer is: Modified - qualified opinion (due to material misstatement).

The inclusion of the receivables balance is a material misstatement in the financial statements. As such, an unmodified report cannot be issued.

The misstatement is not fundamental to a user's understanding of the financial statements, so an adverse opinion is not necessary.

The auditor has been able to obtain sufficient appropriate audit evidence, therefore a qualified opinion stating that the identified misstatement is material but not pervasive (eg "true and fair except for...") should be issued.

2.4   The correct answer is: The auditor obtains sufficient appropriate evidence, but concludes that misstatements are both material and pervasive to the financial statements.

If the auditor concludes the misstatements are material, but not pervasive, then he would issue a qualified opinion.

If he cannot obtain sufficient appropriate evidence to make an opinion, he would issue a disclaimer of opinion.

If he concludes the financial statements are free from material misstatement, he would issue an unmodified opinion.

2.5   The correct answer is: Disclaimer of opinion.

A disclaimer of opinion is required when the auditor has been unable to obtain sufficient appropriate audit evidence and the effect of undetected misstatements is likely to be material and pervasive.

2.6   The correct answer is: Modified - qualified opinion due to material misstatement.

IAS 38 *Intangible assets*, only development expenditure may be capitalised and only if it meets certain criteria. Research costs must be expensed. The capitalisation of the research costs is therefore a material misstatement in the accounts due to non-compliance with IAS 38 and a qualified opinion should be issued.

The misstatement is not fundamental to a user's understanding of the accounts, therefore it is not pervasive and an adverse opinion is not necessary.

An emphasis of matter paragraph is not appropriate because the accounts include a material misstatement.

2.7   The correct answers are:

- A statement of management's and auditor's responsibilities
- A statement of the auditor's opinion as to the truth and fairness of the financial statements
- A statement that the audit was conducted in accordance with International Standards on Auditing
- A statement that the audit includes evaluating the appropriateness of the accounting policies used.

An unmodified audit report does not deal with the going concern status of the company.

2.8   The correct answer is: Qualified opinion.

Qualified opinion should be issued as the amount is material but not pervasive to the financial statements.

2.9   The correct answer are:

- Whether the company has kept proper accounting records

- Whether the financial statements are in agreement with the accounting records

- Whether the financial statements have been prepared in accordance with the relevant legislation and accounting standards

- Whether the other information presented with the financial statements is consistent with them

The auditor's report covers all of these matters.

2.10   The correct answer is: The financial statements have been prepared by a qualified accountant.

In order to state that the financial statements show a true and fair view the auditor must satisfy himself that:

- Proper accounting records have been kept

- The financial statements have been prepared in accordance with local legislation and relevant accounting standards

- The financial statements are in agreement with accounting records

3 Ethics

3.1   The correct answer is: The audit firm giving evidence in court on behalf of the client.

3.2   The correct answer is: Fraud.

Fraud could arise from, or be associated with, one of these threats, but is not in itself a type of threat.

The other type of threat is intimidation.

3.3   The correct answer is: Recruiting senior management for the client.

Recruiting senior management for the client is a possible source of threat to independence.

3.4   The correct answer is: Auditing financial statements.

The audit of the financial statements will be carried out by an accountant in practice.

3.5   The correct answer is: Encourages consistent application of rules.

A principles-based approach sets out principles and guidelines, rather than detailed rules to cover every specific situation. This leads to the listed advantages - but not to consistent application, since there is a high degree of discretion in applying guidelines to different cases.

3.6   The correct answer is: Professional competence and due care, Confidentiality, Integrity.

Reliability, morality and efficiency are not fundamental principles.

3.7   The correct answer is: Self-interest.

If such threats are significant (i.e. the interest is direct and of high value), safeguards will have to be put in place.

3.8   The correct answer is: Professional competence and due care.

This raises issues of professional competence and due care. You know that you do not have the knowledge to answer these questions at this time and in this situation. For your own professional safety, you should make the client clearly aware of this and not be prepared to give any opinion, as this may be relied upon by the client despite the circumstances. The most appropriate form of action would be to make an appointment with

BPP
LEARNING MEDIA

the client to discuss the matter properly after you have done some research into these specific areas, or refer them to a colleague with experience in this area.

3.9 The correct answer is:

- It encourages compliance by requiring a professional person to actively consider the issues.

The other statements all describe the features of a rules-based code.

3.10 The correct answer is: Disclosure of information to advance the interests of a new client.

This would not be permitted under the Code.

4 The Conceptual Framework

4.1 The correct answer is: It is an accounting standard that companies have to comply with.

The IASB's *Conceptual framework for financial reporting* is not an accounting standard, however it is extremely influential for companies preparing and presenting their financial statements.

4.2 The correct answer is: Profits

The Conceptual Framework defines the elements as the broad classes into which the effect of transactions and other events are categorised in the financial statements.

Assets are an element of the financial statements referring to rights or other access to future economic benefits controlled by an entity as a result of past transactions or events.

Liabilities are similar to assets except they are obligations to transfer rather than receive economic benefit.

Equity is the residual interest in the assets of the entity after deducting all its liabilities.

4.3 The correct answers are:

- Similar items within a single set of financial statements should be given similar accounting treatment.
- Similar items should be treated in the same way from one period to the next

These statements describe comparability.

Under the accruals concept, the non-cash effects of transactions should be reflected in the financial statements for the accounting period in which they occur and not in the period where any cash involved is received or paid.

Information is relevant if it has a predictive and / or confirmatory value.

4.4 The correct answer is: It provides a framework for the formulation of accounting standards.

4.5 The correct answers are:

- A coherent conceptual framework can suggest solutions to many issues.
- It helps to reduce the scope for individual judgement and potential subjectivity.
- It demands that accounts contain relevant information.

It helps ensure that solutions to different issues are the right ones and are consistently applied. It provides guidance in areas not subject to accounting standards, which will help make different financial statements more comparable.

This may mean that the legal form of transaction is superseded by the substance of the transaction as required by IAS 1 *Presentation of financial statements*.

Although the Framework document is similar to the US Statement of Principles (issued by FASB in the USA) it is not the same. Also, not all the US GAAP rules are consistent with the US Statement of Principles.

4.6   The correct answers are:

- To assist auditors in forming an opinion regarding whether financial statements conform with IASs/IFRSs.

- It assists the Board of the IASB in the development of future International Financial Reporting Standards and in its review of existing standards.

- It assists national standard setting bodies in developing national standards.

These are specifically stated as purposes of the Framework .

A conceptual framework helps to provide clarity on the fundamental principles governing the preparation and presentation of financial statements, however, it cannot prevent misleading financial statements just as traffic laws don't stop people speeding.

4.7   The correct answers are:

- Relevance.
- Faithful representation.

Relevance and faithful representation are fundamental qualitative characteristics of financial information.

Predictive value is a sub-section of relevance.

Comparability and understandability are two of the four enhancing qualitative characteristics of financial information. The other two are verifiability and timeliness.

Consistency is a sub-section of comparability.

4.8   The correct answer is: The price that would be received to sell an asset or paid to transfer a liability in an orderly transaction between market participants at the measurement date.

The key point is that the transaction is between a willing buyer and seller.

In a forced sale situation, a 'fair value' might not be realised as the seller might not be a willing party to the sale.

4.9   The correct answers are: Profits and Losses.

The elements of financial statements are assets, liabilities and equity in the statement of financial position and income and expenses in the statement of profit or loss and other comprehensive income.

Profits and losses are not elements.

4.10   The correct answer is: Financial performance.

The statement of profit or loss and other comprehensive income measures financial performance. The entity's economic resources and claims are shown in the statement of financial position and financial adaptability is shown in the statement of cash flows.

5 Presentation of published financial statements

5.1   The correct answer is: Finance costs.

Finance costs must be included on the face of the statement of profit or loss.

5.2   The correct answer is: it includes other comprehensive income.

Other comprehensive income is included within the aggregated amount for total comprehensive income.

Changes in equity is a primary statement and includes gains taken directly to reserves.

It is presented with the same prominence as the statement of profit or loss and statement of financial position. All gains are included whether they are reported in the statement of profit or loss or in reserves.

5.3 The correct answer is: $185,000.

Profit for the year (after tax, before dividends) (W1)	110
Unrealised revaluation gain (150-75)	75
Total comprehensive income	185

Working (W1)

Retained earnings (400 – 340)	60
Add back: dividends	50
Profit for year after taxation	110

5.4 The correct answers are:

- The company has material underprovision for income tax arising from the use of incorrect data by the tax advisors acting for the company.

- A deterioration in sales performance has led to the directors restating their methods for the calculation of the general irrecoverable debt provision.

IAS 8 does not permit recurrent adjustments or correction of estimates to be treated as retrospective corrections since these are a normal feature of everyday business accounting practices. In the situation described, if this was a one-off correction of a material error then it would be a retrospective correction.

The restatement of the methods for the calculation of the general irrecoverable debt provision does not appear to be a restatement of the policy for accounting for irrecoverable debts. If the directors could demonstrate the change is material and gives a fairer view of the company's affairs, then perhaps it could be argued that this option is a change in policy.

In general, errors which arose as a result of imperfectly available information will be treated as a change in accounting estimates. Errors that arise as a result of carelessness or negligence will be treated as correction of an error.

5.5 The correct answer is: The impact of disposals is highlighted.

This information comes from complying with IFRS 5.

All of the other options are seen as benefits of segmental disclosures.

5.6 The correct answer is: $36m.

	$m
Profit for the year	29
Revaluations (14 – 7)	7
	36

5.7 The correct answers are:

	$'000
Revenue	1,260
Current assets	361

The amounts are calculated as:

	$'000
Revenue – per trial balance	1,275
Less: deposit on goods not yet despatched	(15)
	1,260

Current assets	
Inventory – per trial balance	186
Receivables – per trial balance	175
	361

5.8   The correct answer is: 629

The amounts are calculated as:

	$'000
Cost of sales - per trial balance	554
Depreciation of plant and equipment:	
P&E with a revised useful life - (120 – [120 × 12.5% × 4 years]) = 60 ÷ 2 years	30
Other P&E - (480 – 120) × 12.5%	45
	629

5.9   The correct answers are:

	$'000
Administrative expenses	201
Finance charge	14

The amounts are calculated as:

	$'000
Administrative expenses – per trial balance	180
Building depreciation: (960 – 260) × 3%	21
	201
Finance charge – per trial balance	7
Interest accrual (280 × 5%) – 7	7
	14

5.10   The correct answers are:

	$'000
Tax expense	62
Current tax payable	52
Share capital	560
Share premium	120

The amounts are calculated as:

	$'000
Tax expense	
Charge for the year	52
Current tax payable	10
	62
Current tax payable	52
Share capital – per trial balance	560
Share premium – per trial balance	120

6 Non-current assets I

6.1   The correct answers are:

- Directly attributable labour costs.
- A reasonable proportion of indirect costs.
- Interest on capital borrowed to finance production of the asset.

Labour costs directly attributable to producing the asset are part of its total cost of production.

Production costs may include a reasonable proportion of indirect costs.

Interest incurred on capital borrowed to finance production of the asset is a relevant production cost when a company is constructing an asset for its own consumption.

6.2   The correct answers are:

- For a purchased asset, expenses incidental (directly attributable) to the acquisition of the asset
- For a manufactured asset, direct costs of production plus a reasonable proportion of indirect costs.

For a purchased asset, expenses incidental to the acquisition of the asset and the direct costs and a reasonable proportion of the indirect costs of a manufactured asset can be included in the calculation of the cost of a non-current asset.

6.3 The correct answer is:

- Dr Accumulated depreciation $20,000, Dr Property at cost $30,000, Cr Revaluation surplus $50,000.

Dr Accumulated depreciation $20,000

Dr Property at cost $30,000

Cr Revaluation surplus $50,000

All depreciation to date must be eliminated.

The original cost is increased to the revalued amount

6.4 The correct answer is: A method that allocates the depreciable amount as fairly as possible.

IAS 16 does not prescribe any specific method.

6.5 The correct answer is: $38,000.

CA (30 September 20X6)	=	40,000
	=	80%
CA (30 September 20X5)	=	(40,000 × 100)/ 80
	=	50,000
CA (30 September 20X4)	=	(50,000 × 100)/80
	=	62,500
Cost (1 October 20X3)	=	(62,500 × 100)/80
	=	78,125
Accumulated depreciation	=	$78,125 – $40,000
	=	$38,000

6.6 The correct answer is: Initial operating losses while the production plant reaches planned performance.

Per IAS 16, this should be treated as an expense, not part of an asset. The other costs are all directly attributable to bringing the asset into operation. As the lease of the building expires after 10 years, the costs of dismantling are included.

6.7 The correct answer is: Capitalised and depreciated over the period to the next inspection.

The cost should not be accrued for or provided for. The inspection is treated as an additional component, so it is capitalised and depreciated.

6.8 The correct answer is: $31,600.

This is calculated as:

	$
Original purchase price	50,000
Depreciation 20X1: (50,000 – 5,000)/5	(9,000)
Depreciation 20X2	(9,000)
Upgrade	15,000
	47,000
Depreciation 20X3: (47,000 – 5,000)/5	(8,400)
Carrying amount 1 January 20X4	38,600
Disposal proceeds	(7,000)
Loss on disposal	31,600

6.9   The correct answer is: $1,055,000.

	$
Purchase price	780,000
Import duties	117,000
Site preparation costs	30,000
Installation costs	28,000
Estimated cost of dismantling and removal of the asset, required to be recognised as a provision	100,000
	1,055,000

6.10   The correct answer is:

- An allocation of EW's administration costs, based on EW staff time spent on the construction as a percentage of the total staff time.

Administration costs would not be included as these do not relate specifically to the non-current asset.

7 Non-current assets II

7.1   The correct answers are:

An investment property is:
- An investment in land and/or buildings.
- Held for its investment potential.
- Not occupied by the reporting entity for its own purposes.

An investment property is a special category of land and buildings. Any rental income should be negotiated at arms length. A company (or related group company) cannot occupy an investment property.

7.2   The correct answer is: In other comprehensive income as a revaluation gain.

This gain arose during the period before the property was reclassified, so it is accounted for under IAS 16. It will be shown in the statement of changes in equity as an addition to the revaluation surplus. Any subsequent gains will be accounted for under IAS 40 and recognised in profit or loss. This a revaluation gain, not investment income.

7.3   The correct answers are:

- One method of accounting for capital grants is to reduce the acquisition cost of the non-current asset by the amount of the grant and charging depreciation on the reduced amount

- Grants relating to income are a credit to profit or loss and these may be deducted from related expenses

There are only two (not three) permitted ways of accounting for a government grant.

The final profit figure will be the same however government grants are accounted for.

An entity should not recognise a government grant until it has reasonable assurance that it will comply with conditions attached.

7.4   The correct answer is: $3,062,500.

This is calculated using the weighted average of the borrowing costs applicable to Z Co's general borrowings as no specific funds were borrowed for asset Y. This is calculated as follows:

Weighted cost of capital   = $(8\% \times 100/(100 + 60)) + (10\% \times 60 + (100+ 60))$
                           = $5\% + 3.75\%$
                           = 8.75%

Borrowing costs   = $(\$20m \times 8.75\%) + (\$30m \times 8.75\% \times (6/12))$
                  = $\$(1,750,000 + 1,312,500)$
                  = $\$3,062,500$

7.5   The correct answer is: $27,050,000.

Although the loan carries no interest as such, the premium on the repayment represents a borrowing cost and this should be allocated to accounting periods over the term of the loan at a constant rate on the carrying amount.

The effective rate of interest is 10% and is applied to the loan amount as follows:

	B/f $m	Interest $m	C/f $m
20X3	100	10.0	110.00
20X4	110	11.0	121.00
20X5	121	12.1	133.10

Interest can be capitalised only during the time that construction is in progress. Three of the apartments are completed at 30 September 20X4; therefore only 50% of the interest for 20X5 can be capitalised as part of the cost of the development.

Therefore total capitalised = 10 + 11 + 6.05 = 27.05.

7.6   The correct answers are:

Investment property depreciation $0
Gain on investment property $200,000

Investment properties valued under the fair value model are not depreciated instead the investment property is remeasured at fair value at the end of the period.

7.7   The correct answers are:

- The standard requires grants to be recognised as income over the relevant periods to match them with the related costs which they have received to compensate.

- An entity should recognise government grants as soon as it has reasonable assurance that the entity will actually receive the grant

7.8   The correct answers are:

Annual Profit after depreciation $562,500
Carrying amount of the asset in year 3 $187,500

Carrying amount of asset in year 3 = (Non-current asset $400,000 – 25% grant $100,000) – (3 years × $37,500 depreciation) = $187,500

7.9   The correct answers are:

- A qualifying asset is an asset that takes a substantial period of time to get ready for its intended use or sale.

- Borrowing costs are defined as interest and other costs incurred by the entity in connection with the borrowing of funds.

Borrowing costs MUST be capitalised under IAS 23, not expensed (unless there are periods of interruption)

Investment income must be netted against borrowing costs in the statement of financial position.

7.10   The correct answer is:

- Financial assets and inventories that are manufactured, or otherwise produced over a short period of time are qualifying assets.

These are NOT qualifying assets since the asset should be constructed over a substantial period of time.

8 Non-current assets III

8.1 The correct answers are:

- Purchased goodwill is written off immediately against reserves.

- Internally generated brands are capitalised at fair value as advised by independent consultants.

- In calculating depreciation, the estimated useful life of an asset is taken as half the actual estimated useful life as a measure of prudence.

Purchased goodwill must be capitalised on the statement of financial position and reviewed annually for impairment; land should not be depreciated; internally generated brands cannot be capitalised and the useful life of an asset is the period over which the entity expects to generate future economic benefit from the asset.

8.2 The correct answer is:

- GHK spent $12,000 researching a new type of product. The research is expected to lead to a new product line in 3 years' time.

Research expenditure can never be capitalised and must be recognised as an expense in the statement of profit or loss in accordance with IAS 38.

8.3 The correct answer is: $56,000.

The $12,000 spent on converting seaweed does not meet the recognition criteria for an intangible asset and so must be recognised as an expense in profit or loss.

The $60,000 relating to the headache pill must be capitalised. Amortisation must start once commercial production begins and amortisation is $1,000 per month ($60,000 / 5 years).

The value at the year end represents $60,000 less four months amortisation.

8.4 The correct answer is: $35,000.

The $27,000 research costs are not directed towards a confirmed outcome and so should be recognised as an expense. The $8,000 market research costs suggest that the commercial viability of the product has not yet been determine and so the capitalisation criteria have not yet been satisfied.

9 Impairment of assets

9.1 The correct answer is: The operating performance of the machine has declined.

Market values and technological changes are external factors. The machine being fully depreciated does not mean it is impaired.

9.2 The correct answer is: $22,000.

The recoverable amount is the higher of the value in use of the asset and the asset's fair value less costs to sell (i.e. the net realisable value of the asset).

9.3 The correct answer is:

$200,000   Recognised in other comprehensive income

On 30 September 20X4 the building was revalued upwards by $900,000 and the gain on revaluation was taken to the revaluation surplus:

Revaluation surplus at 30 Sept 20X4 = $1.8m −($1m − ($1m × 2/20))
= $900,000

Therefore IAS 36 *Impairment of assets* states that the impairment loss of $200,000 ($1.7m − 1.5m) should be charged against the previous revaluation surplus of $900,000 leaving a revaluation surplus of $700,000 and a carrying amount for the building of $1,500,000.

Carrying amount of building at 30 Sept 20X5   = $1.8m − ($1m/18)

                                                    = $1.7m

Market value at 30 Sept 20X5   = $1.5m

9.4   The correct answer is: Nil.

The recoverable amount of the machine (higher of fair value less costs to sell and value in use) is $150,000. This is higher than carrying amount so the machine is not impaired.

9.5   The correct answer is: $1,500

The carrying amount of the machine at 30 September 20X5 is $10,500 ($21,000 / 6 years × 3 years).

The recoverable amount of the asset at 30 September 20X5 is $9,000. This is the higher of the asset's fair value less costs to sell ($9,200 − $500) and its value in use ($9,000).

Therefore the impairment loss is $1,500 ($10,500 − $9,000).

9.6   The correct answer is: $50,000.

At 30 September 20X5 the brand has a carrying amount of $250,000.

Revaluation surplus at 30 Sept 20X4 = $500,000 − ($500,000 × 5/10)
                                                 = $250,000

IAS 36 requires the brand to be written down to its recoverable amount, which is the higher of its fair value less costs to sell and value in use.

Therefore the recoverable amount is the market value of $200,000 as this is higher than its value in use of $150,000.

Thus there is an impairment loss of $50,000 ($250,000 − $200,000) which is recognised immediately in the statement of profit or loss and other comprehensive income.

The brand is measured at $200,000 in the statement of financial position and reported as an intangible asset.

10 Reporting financial performance I

10.1   The correct answer is: $730,000.

The asset should be classified as held for sale and valued at the lower of its carrying amount ($750,000) and its fair value less costs to sell ($740,000 − $10,000).

Note that non-current assets held for sale are not depreciated.

10.2   The correct answer is: Under current assets.

Non-current assets held for sale are shown separately under the 'current assets' heading.

10.3   The correct answer is: Disclose the machine separately from other property, plant and equipment and no longer depreciate it.

The machine will be presented under 'Non-current assets held for sale'.

10.4   The correct answer is:

- After tax results of North American operation, including any profit or loss on disposal, shown as a one-line entry 'profit/ loss from discontinued operation'.

10.5 The correct answer is: $370 million.

The airline operation was sold before the year end and was a distinguishable component of the entity and is therefore a discontinued operation as defined by IFRS 5 *Non-current assets held for sale and discontinued operations.*

A separate line in the statement of profit or loss and other comprehensive income for discontinued operations should be included after the profit after tax for continuing operations. IFRS 5 states that this should be made up of the post-tax profit or loss of the discontinued operation ($100 million) and the post-tax gain or loss on disposal of the airline assets. The loss on sale of the fleet of aircraft of $250m and the provision for severance payments of $20m will both be reported in this line.

The $10 million costs relating to the restructuring will be reported as part of the continuing activities, probably as part of administrative expenses. They are not included within the amount for discontinued operations.

10.6 The correct answers are:

- The sale price must be at at least its fair value
- The sale must have been agreed at the end of the reporting period but need not have been completed

The IFRS 5 criteria are:

- It must be available for immediate sale in its present condition
- The sale must be highly probable (this indicates that a reasonable price must be being charged but the standard does not specify anything relating to fair value)
- The entity must be actively seeking a sale and committed to selling it
- The sale should be expected to be complete within one year of it being classified as held for sale

10.7 The correct answer is: $12,000.

The scenario provides the carrying amounts of the assets at the beginning of the period, i.e. at 31 March 20X0. The outlet was classified as held for sale on 31 March 20X1 and so the assets need to be depreciated for the period from 1 April 20X0 to 31 March 20X1.

This is calculated as:

	Carrying amount at 1 April 20X0	Dep'n charge for 20X1	Carrying amount at 31 March 20X1
	$'000	$'000	$'000
Land (no dep'n)	150	0	150
Buildings	20	40 (cost) × 5% = 2	18
Plant and Equipment	25	25(CA) × 20% = 5	20
	195		188

Therefore the assets have a carrying amount of $188,000 at 31 March 20X1.

When they are classified as held for sale they must be valued and the lower of the current carrying amount ($188,000) and the fair value less costs to sell ($176,000).

Therefore there is an impairment loss of $12,000 ($188,000 - $176,000).

10.8 The correct answer is: $375,000.

At 31 December 20X3 the carrying amount of the machine is:

Cost	600,000
Depreciation (600,000 × 3 years 9 months/ 10 years)	(225,000)
	375,000

This is lower than fair value less costs to sell ($400,000).

Note that the asset is only depreciated up to 1 October 20X3 when it is classified as held for sale.

The asset's value in use is irrelevant as the machine is to be sold.

10.9 The correct answer is: Profit or loss after tax, including gain or loss on disposal.

IFRS 5 requires disclosure of a single amount on the face of the statement of profit or loss. This single amount should be analysed in the notes into:

(a) Revenue, expenses and pre-paid tax or loss of discontinued operations.
(b) The related income tax expense.
(c) The gain or loss recognised on disposal of the assets or the discontinued operation.
(d) The related income tax expense.

10.10 The correct answers are:

- Sale or closure must be completed by the end of the reporting period.
- The anticipated sale is an associate acquired exclusively with a view to resale.

Sale or closure does not have to occur by the year end for the operation to be treated as discontinued.

A discontinued operation can be a subsidiary acquired exclusively with a view to resale, not an associate.

11 Reporting financial performance II

11.1 The correct answers are:

- The presentation currency of an entity is selected by management.
- The functional currency of an entity is identified by reference to circumstances of the business.

11.2 The correct answer is:

- Added to the tax expense in the statement of profit or loss.

Tax underestimated in the previous year will already have been paid to the tax authorities, so it is not added to the current tax payable figure in the statement of financial position.

However, it is added to the tax charge in the statement of profit or loss.

11.3 The correct answer is:

Statement of profit or loss $256,000; Statement of financial position $240,000.

	$
Current tax payable	
(800,000 × 30%)	240,000
Under-provision re previous year	16,000
Statement of profit or loss tax expense	256,000

11.4 The correct answers are:

- The $150,000 dividend was shown in the notes to the financial statements at 31 October 20X5.

- The dividend is shown as a deduction in the statement of changes in equity for the year ended 31 October 20X6.

The dividend was not declared before 31 October 20X5 and so cannot be recognised during that year. Instead it should be disclosed in a note to the financial statements at 31 October 20X5.

The dividend will be recognised in the statement of changes in equity in the year ended 31 October 20X6.

11.5 The correct answers are:

- A material event that occurs before the financial statements are authorised that provides more evidence of conditions that already existed at the reporting date should be adjusted for in the financial statements.

- The notes to the financial statements must give details of non-adjusting events affecting the users' ability to understand the company's financial position.

- Financial statements should not be prepared on a going concern basis if after the end of the reporting period but before the financial statements are authorised the directors have decided to liquidate the company.

All three statements are correct.

11.6 The correct answers are:

- Monetary assets and liabilities should be restated at the closing rate.
- Non-monetary assets and liabilities should not be restated.

11.7 The correct answer is: $48,000.

This is calculated as:

	$
Provision for current period	50,000
Over provision for prior period	(2,000)
Total charge to tax for the year	48,000

11.8 The correct answer is: $30,200.

This is calculated as:

	$
Provision for current period	30,000
Under provision for prior period	200
Charge to SPL	30,200

11.9 The correct answer is: $1,664,000.

This is calculated as:

	$
Profit before tax	1,800,000
Fall in investment value (non-adjusting event)	0
Write down of receivable	(116,000)
Inventory write down (161 – 141)	20,000)
Seizure of assets (non-adjusting event)	0
	1,664,000

11.10 The correct answer is:

- On 1 October 20X8, GD made a rights issue of 1 new share for every 3 shares held at a price of $175. The market price on that date was $200.

An adjusting event is an event that provides further evidence of a condition that already existed at the reporting date.

A non-adjusting event relates to the situation where the condition did not exist at the reporting date.

12 Employee benefits

12.1 The correct answer is:

- IAS 19 requires all re-measurement gains and losses each year to be reported in other comprehensive income.

12.2 The correct answer is:

- Once they have paid their contributions the company's liability is met.

The other statements are true of a defined benefit scheme.

12.3 The correct answer is:

- The pension payable to an employee is calculated by reference to the salary earned in the qualifying period prior to retirement.

There is no guarantee that the fund will meet pension commitments, it is the role of the actuary to determine the adequacy of the fund and to recommend adjustments.

The contributions will vary because of changes in the scheme assumptions and funding.

The accruals concept applies to equalise fund charges to the statement of profit or loss, therefore there may be pension fund prepayments or provisions.

12.4 The correct answer is: $610,000.

$20 million plus bonus of $6 million = $26 million × 6% = $1,560,000.

$1,560,000 – $950,000 = $610,000.

12.5 The correct answer is: Current service cost + net interest on net defined asset/liability + past service cost.

Re-measurement gains/losses are recognised in other comprehensive income.

Contributions paid increase plan assets and reduce bank.;

Benefits paid to former employees reduce both the plan assets and plan liabilities.

12.6 The correct answers are:

- Defined contribution scheme.
- Defined benefit scheme.

A money purchase scheme is often used as a synonym for defined contribution scheme, but this is not the term used by IAS 19. A company pension scheme is a vague term: it could be either defined contribution or defined benefit.

12.7 The correct answer is: $165,000

	$
Opening defined benefit obligation	6,600,00
Current service cost	875,000
Benefits paid	(650,000)
Increase in PV of liabilities	540,000
Re-measurement gain(balancing figure)	(165,000)
Closing defined benefit obligation	7,200,000

12.8 The correct answer is: $6,300,000.

	$
Fair value of plan assets at 1 January 20X2	5,700,000
Interest on b/d assets at 4%	228,000
Benefits paid to past employees	(280,000)
Contributions paid	820,000
Re-measurement loss on plan assets	(168,000)
Fair value of plan assets at 31 December 20X2	6,300,000

12.9 The correct answer is: $665,000.

	$
Current service cost	650,000
Interest on b/d assets (5% × $2,700,000)	(135,000)
Interest on b/d liabilities (5% × $3,000,000)	150,000
Expense	665,000

12.10 The correct answer is:

- A change in the actuarial assumptions in respect of the valuation of the present value of the pension plan's obligations.

13 Statement of cashflows

13.1 The correct answer is: Repayment of an overdraft.

An overdraft is a borrowing facility repayable on demand. The repayment of an overdraft will increase the amount of cash which is the bottom line of the statement of cash flows and will be included in the increase or decrease in cash and cash equivalents for the year.

The issue of ordinary shares would be a cash inflow under 'financing'.

The repurchase of a long-term loan means the company is paying the loan back and this would be a cash outflow under 'financing'.

Dividends paid can be shown as an outflow in either the operating activities section or in the financing outflow section of the statement of cash flows.

13.2 The correct answer is: The statement of profit or loss charge for taxation for the current year.

The profit or loss charge is not shown in the statement of cash flows, rather the statement of cash flows will show the actual tax paid.

13.3 The correct answer is: Entirely excluded.

Revaluations have no cash flow implications.

13.4 The correct answer is: The statement of profit or loss charge for depreciation for the year.

Depreciation is a non-cash item and so does not appear as a cash outflow. It is added back to the profit before tax figure as a non-cash item when preparing the statement of cash flows under the indirect method.

13.5 The correct answer is: $520,000.

	$'000
Share capital increase (1,600 – 1,200)	400
Share premium increase (400 – 280)	120
	520

13.6 The correct answer is: $38,000.

Interest payable working

	$m
Balance b/d	12,000
Finance charge per SPLOCI	41,000
	53,000
Cash paid (balancing figure)	(38,000)
Balance c/d	15,000

Alternative working:

INTEREST PAYABLE

	$		$
Cash paid (bal figure)	38,000	Balance c/d	12,000
Balance c/d	15,000		31,000
	53,000		53,000

13.7 The correct answers are:

- Cash at a bank

- Bank overdraft

- Current asset investments readily convertible into known amounts of cash and which can be sold without disrupting the company's business.

Cash at bank and a bank overdraft would be deemed to be cash whereas current asset investments readily convertible into known amounts of cash would be considered to be cash equivalents.

Equity investments do not generally fulfil the description of cash equivalents.

13.8 The correct answers are:

- Proposed dividends
- Bonus issue of shares
- Surplus on revaluation of a non-current asset

Proposed dividends, a bonus issue of shares and the revaluation of a non-current asset are all non-cash transactions and so would not appear in the statement of cash flows.

13.9 The correct answer is: Profit on sale of non-current asset.

When a non-current asset is disposed of at a profit the profit (or gain) increases the profit before tax figure. This is a non-cash item and so must be deducted when deriving the figure for cash from operating activities.

The amortisation charge for the year is a non-cash item which reduces the profit before tax figure and so this is added back. The surplus on the revaluation of property is also a non-cash item. This does not however impact the profit before tax and so is excluded from the statement of cash flows. A loan repayment is shown as a cash outflow in the financing section of the statement of cash flows.

13.10 The correct answer is:

- Cash flows from operating activities reconciliation: $(9,000); Cash inflow: $30,000.

The $9,000 profit is shown before profit before tax in the statement of profit or loss. As it is not a cash flow it is deducted from the profit before tax figure in the reconciliation of profit before tax to net cash from operating activities.

The cash received was $30,000 and this is an inflow under the heading of cash flows from investing activities.

14 The consolidated statement of financial position I

14.1 Feedback The correct answer is: Annually.

IFRS 3 Business Combinations states that goodwill acquired in a business combination should be reviewed for impairment annually.

14.2 The correct answer is:

The subsidiary has been acquired exclusively with a view to subsequent disposal.

Exclusion for dissimilar activities is not permitted because adequate information should be available via the disclosures required by IFRS 8 Segment reporting.

14.3 The correct answer is: EF Only.

Only AB has 40% of the voting rights and 80% of the non-voting rights in CD; therefore AB does not have control of CD.

AB has a minority of the voting rights (40%) of EF but it has control in that it has the power to appoint and remove directors, therefore EF is a subsidiary of AB.

14.4 The correct answer is: $24,800.

	$
NCI at acquisition at fair value	14,800
NCI share of post-acquisition reserves 25% ($115,000 – $65,000)	12,500
Less NCI share of impairment losses (25% × $10,000)	(2,500)
	24,800

14.5 The correct answer is: $131,250.

	$
NCI at acquisition 25% × ($310,000 + $165,000)	118,750
NCI share of post-acquisition reserves 25% × ($215,000 – $165,000)	12,500
	131,250

14.6 The correct answer is: Carried at cost, with an annual impairment review.

14.7 The correct answer is: $3.04 million.

	$'m
Non-controlling interest at acquisition 40% × ($4.4m + $2.3m)	2.68
Non-controlling interest share of post-acquisition reserves 40% × ($3.2m – $2.3m)	0.36
	3.04

14.8 The correct answer is: $2.46 million.

	$'m
Non-controlling interest at acquisition at fair value	2.3
NCI share of post-acquisition reserves 10% × ($7.9m – $6.3m)	0.16
	2.46

14.9 The correct answer is: $96.4 million.

	TR $m	SD $m
Per question	81	54
Pre-acquisition		(32)
		22

Group share of post-acquisition revaluation surplus (70% × $22m)	15.4
Consolidated revaluation surplus	96.4

14.10 The correct answer is: $223,200.

	QZ $	FT $
Per question ($140,000 + $80,000)/($60,000 + $40,000)	220,000	100,000
Pre-acquisition		(60,000)
		40,000
Group share of post-acquisition reserves (80% × $40,000)	32,000	
Less group share of impairment loss (80% × $36,000)	(28,800)	
Consolidated retained earnings	223,200	

15 The consolidated statement of financial position II

15.1 The correct answer is:

- Deduct $6,000 from consolidated receivables and $4,000 from consolidated payables, and include cash in transit of $2,000.

You need to account for cash in transit.

15.2 The correct answer is: $80,500.

	$
NCI at acquisition	48,000
NCI share of post-acquisition reserves	32,500
25% × ($520,000 – $370,000 – $20,000 (W1)	
	80,500

W1

	$
Less proportion depreciated by year end ($25,000 × 1/5)	25,000
Less proportion depreciated by year end ($25,000 × 1/5)	(5,000)
Adjust G's retained earnings	20,000

15.3 The correct answer is:

Dr Retained earnings of YZ $1,500, Cr Consolidated inventory $1,500.

Dr Retained earnings of YZ (33⅓/133⅓ x $6,000) $1,500, Cr Consolidated inventory $1,500.

15.4 The correct answer is: $2,632,000.

	BV $000	JK $000
At 31 December 20X6	2,560	880
Pre-acquisition retained earnings (W1)		(784)
		96
Group share (75% × $96,000)	72	
Consolidated retained earnings	2,632	

W1

	$000
At 31 December 20X6	880
Less profit for the year	(144)
At 1 January 20X6	736
Add profit to 1 May 20X6 ($144,000 × 4/12)	48
Retained earnings of JK at 1 May 20X6	784

15.5 The correct answer is:

- Remove $7.8 million from revenue and cost of sales. Increase cost of sales and reduce inventory by the profit on the goods remaining in inventory at the year end.

15.6 The correct answer is: $80,000.

$100,000 sales in transit include a mark-up of 25% which needs to be eliminated. Sales at cost, excluding the mark-up are therefore ($100,000 × 100%)/125% = $80,000.

15.7 The correct answer is: $3,100 to be included as cash in transit.

The payment sent by STV the holding company to its subsidiary TUW should be included as cash in transit on consolidation.

15.8 The correct answer is:

Reduce group inventory by $10,000 and reduce parent's profits by $10,000 to eliminate the unrealised profit in inventory.

This is because the parent made the sale. The adjustment is $10,000 which is (20% x $100,000 x 50%).

15.9 The correct answer is: $9,600.

The carrying amount at transfer was:
$10,000 − (5 × $1,000) = $5,000

Unrealised profit on the transaction was:
$17,000 − $5,000 = $12,000

Less proportion depreciated by the year end:
$12,000 / 5 = $2,400

The net reduction of group profit is thus:
$12,000 − $2,400 = $9,600

15.10 The correct answer is: $3,296,000.

	MX $000	FZ $000
At 31 December 20X9	3,200	1,100
Less unrealised profit (W1)		(60)
Pre-acquisition retained earnings		(920)
		120
Group share (80% × $120,000)	96	
Consolidated retained earnings	3,296	

W1

Intra group sales by FZ $300,000

Margin ($300,000 × 20%) = $60,000 (adjust FZ's retained earnings as FZ make sale)

16 The consolidated statement of profit of loss and other comprehensive income

16.1 The correct answer is: $175,000.

	$
Pumpkin	100,000
Squash	80,000
	180,000
Less intra-group sales	(8,000)
Add provision for unrealised profit (8,000 – 5,000)	3,000
	175,000

16.2 The correct answer is:

- Dr Revenue $100,000; Cr Cost of sales $100,000.

Intra-group revenue must be eliminated in full from revenue as income and costs are wholly intra-group. As there is no unsold inventory at the year end and, therefore, no unrealised profit, the adjustment to costs is the same as the adjustment to revenue.

16.3 The correct answer is:

	Dr	Cr
Group revenue	$28,000	
Group cost of sales		$28,000
Being removal of intra group trading		
YZ Cost of sales (W1)	$1,500	
Group inventory		$1,500
Being removal of unrealised profit		

W1

Profit on goods held at year end $6,000 × 33⅓/133⅓ = $1,500

16.4 The correct answer is:

Group Profit	*Non-controlling interest*
Reduced by $3,000	Reduced by $2,000

The provision for unrealised profit is $5,000 ($30,000 20/120).

The subsidiary has sold to the parent; therefore the unrealised profit has arisen in the accounts of the subsidiary and must be allocated between the group and the non controlling interest.

16.5 The correct answer is: $100.

	$
Profit attributable:	
Owners of the parent (balancing figure)	5,000
Non-controlling interest 20% × ($1,100 – $600)	100
Profit for the year ($4,600 + $1,100 – $600)	5,100

16.6 The correct answer is: $7,650,000.

	$000
Profit attributable to:	
Owners of parent (balancing figure)	7,650
Non-controlling interest (30% ×$1,980,000)	594
Consolidated profit for the year ($7,020,000 + $1,980,000) – $756,000	8,244

17 Associates

17.1 The correct answer is: Admiral and Sultan.

Consul cannot exercise significant influence over Warrior because it is controlled by another company. However, it has the largest shareholdings and a board seat, so exercising significant influence, over Admiral. Sultan is not so clear. As another entity also has significant influence over it is likely that Consul does too.

17.2 The correct answer is: $16,250.

	$
Share of profit of associate	
25% × $100,000 × 9 ÷ 12	18,750
Unrealised profit (W1)	(2,500)
	16,250

EF (associate) sells to AB (parent)

$80,000 × 25% × ½ = $10,000

Group share $10,000 × 25% = $2,500 deducted from 'share of associate profit'

17.3 The correct answer is: $1,400,000.

Group profit for the period includes the group's share of the profit of the associate.

	$'000
Savoy	700
Spring	550
White (30% × $500)	150
	1,400

17.4 The correct answer is: $3,000.

	$
Profit on sale ($160,000 ÷ 4)	40,000
Unrealised profit on sale ($40,000 × 25%)	10,000
Group share (30% × 10,000)	3,000

18 General principles of taxation

18.1 The correct answer is:

- Tax evasion is the illegal manipulation of the tax system to avoid paying taxes due. Tax avoidance is tax planning, legally arranging affairs so as to minimise the tax liability.

Tax evasion is a way of paying less tax by illegal methods whereas tax avoidance is a way of arranging your affairs to take advantage of the tax rules to pay as little tax as possible, and is legal.

18.2 The correct answer is:

- The difference between the total amount of tax due to be paid and the amount actually collected by the tax authority.

The tax gap is the gap between the tax theoretically collectable and the amount actually collected.

18.3 The correct answer is:

- It should raise as much money as possible for the government.

A 'good tax' should be convenient, equitable, certain and efficient according to Adam Smith's canons of taxation.

18.4 The correct answer is: Power of arrest.

Tax authorities have the power to:

- Review and query returns submitted to them.
- Request special reports or returns.
- Examine records which support the returns which have been made.
- Enter and search a business.

18.5 The correct answer is: To ensure tax is paid early.

Setting deadlines is unlikely to result in the early payment of taxes however it will allow tax payers to know the date by which they need to have paid their taxes; tax authorities to forecast the timing of tax receipts and give a point of reference after which penalties can be levied.

18.6 The correct answers are:

- Imprecise and vague tax laws
- Very high tax rates

Imprecise and vague tax laws mean that individuals or companies may consider it easier to try to find tax loopholes, and therefore the incidence of tax evasion and avoidance may increase.

High tax rates mean high tax bills for individuals and companies, and therefore may increase the incentive to avoid or evade paying tax in order to reduce costs.

18.7 The correct answer is: Formal incidence.

Formal incidence describes the individual/ entity that has direct contact with the tax authorities whereas effective incidence describes the individual/ entity that bears the end cost of a tax. Here the effective incidence is on B's customers.

18.8 The correct answer is: The person or entity that finally bears the cost of the tax.

Formal incidence describes the individual/ entity that has direct contact with the tax authorities. However the effective incidence describes the individual/ entity that bears the end cost of a tax.

18.9 The correct answer is: Power to detain company officials.

Tax authorities have the power to:
- Review and query returns submitted to them
- Request special reports or returns
- Examine records which support the returns which have been made
- Enter and search a business

18.10 The correct answer is: The tax authority whose tax laws apply to an entity.

Tax jurisdiction refers to the power of a tax authority to charge and collect tax. The competent jurisdiction is the country whose tax laws apply to the entity.

19 Direct taxation

19.1 The correct answer is: $12,000.

	$
Sale:	
Selling price	450,000
Charges	(15,000)
	435,000
Less purchase:	

Cost	375,000	
Fees	12,000	
		387,000
Profit		48,000
Tax ($48,000 × 25%)		12,000

19.2 The correct answer is:

- It benefits the tax payer as it reduces the tax payable.

The tax payable is the same regardless as to whether it is collected by PAYE or in one lump sum.

19.3 The correct answer is:

- Individual income tax, usually deducted at source.
- Corporate income tax.

Direct taxes are imposed on the income of individuals and the profits made by companies. Import duties and value added tax are examples of indirect taxes.

19.4 The correct answer is: $23,000.

	$
Profit for the year (excluding depreciation)	128,000
Tax depreciation ($72,000 × 50%)	(36,000)
Taxable profit	92,000
Tax at 25%	23,000

19.5 The correct answer is:

Pay $40,000 tax for the year and have no loss to carry forward.

The entity's taxable profits of $480,000 would be reduced by the $320,000 tax losses brought forward. The entity would then have a taxable profit of $160,000 on which tax of $40,000 (25%) would be due. All of the tax losses brought forward would have been used and there would be no loss to carry forward.

19.6 The correct answer is: A classical system.

Here the entity and the shareholder have been treated completely separately for the purpose of calculating tax. This is the classical system.

19.7 The correct answer is: $121,750.

	$
Accounting profit	500,000
Entertaining expenses	51,000
Political donation	36,000
Non-taxable income	(100,000)
Taxable profit	487,000
Tax at 25%	121,750

19.8 The correct answers are:

- It enables tax to be saved at the highest marginal rate.
- It improves the cash flow of the group by enabling the trading loss to be used as soon as possible.

19.9 The correct answer is: $15,000.

This is calculated as follows:

	$
Purchase price of asset	420,000
Add: import duties	30,000
	450,000
Indexation allowance (450,000 × 40%)	180,000
	630,000
Selling price less selling costs (700,000 − 10,000)	(690,000)
Capital gain on disposal	60,000
Tax payable ($60,000 × 25%)	15,000

19.10 The correct answer is: A balancing charge of $850.

The entity has received tax depreciation of $3,750 on the asset ([$6,000 × 50%] + [$6,000 − $3,000] × 25%).

However the asset has only fallen in value by $2,900 ($6,000 − $3,100).

Therefore on disposal there will be a balancing charge of $850 ($3,750 − $2,900).

20 International and indirect taxation

20.1 The correct answer is:

- Tax deducted at source before payment of interest or dividends.

Withholding tax is a tax which is deducted and paid over to the local tax authority before funds (such as dividends and royalties) can be remitted overseas.

20.2 The correct answer is:

- To mitigate taxing overseas income twice

Double taxable treaties deal with overseas income.

20.3 The correct answer is: Specific unit tax.

This is a specific unit tax as it is a charge on each unit (litre) of a specific product (imported petroleum products).

The answer cannot be a general consumption tax because the tax applies to a particular product only, and is therefore not 'general'.

Ad valorem taxes are based on the value of the items, for example a sales tax or value added tax.

20.4 The correct answers are:

- An Indirect tax.
- Formal incidence.

Sales tax is an indirect tax as it is a tax on expenditure (or 'consumption'). The entity has direct contact with the tax authorities and so the formal incidence is on the entity.

20.5 The correct answer is: $50,000.

Sales excluding VAT ($138,000 × 100/115)	120,000
Cost of goods	(70,000)
Profit	50,000

20.6 The correct answer is:

- Corporate income tax is paid on profits remitted by the branch.

Corporate income tax is due on all profits of the branch, not just those remitted.

20.7 The correct answer is: $5,550.

This is calculated as:

	$
Cost	14,000
Excise duty	3,000
	17,000
VAT @ 15%	2,550
	19,550

Taxes paid = $3,000 + $2,550 = $5,550.

20.8 The correct answer is: $0.

Tax paid in Country A:

WHT: 12,000
ULT: $40,000

Tax due in Country B:

	$
Gross dividend	80,000
Add: underlying tax	40,000
	120,000
Tax at 30%	36,000
Less: DTR for WHT	(12,000)
Less: DTR for ULT(capped at $24,000)	(24,000)
Tax payable	0*

*Tax credit cannot create a refund of tax

20.9 The correct answer is: $28,500.

Input tax attributable to exempt outputs cannot be reclaimed. Input tax attributable to zero-rate outputs can be reclaimed, because these outputs are considered to be taxable, but at the zero rate.

20.10 The correct answer is: $12,000.

Output tax 264,500/115 × 15	34,500
Input tax (170,000 − 20,000) × 15%	22,500
Payable	12,000

21 Working capital and the operating cycle

21.1 The correct answer is: An aggressive policy.

Three possible policies exist to finance working capital.

- Conservative policy - all of the permanent assets (current and non-current) and some of the fluctuating current assets are financed by long-term funding.

- Aggressive policy - all of the fluctuating and part of the permanent current assets are financed by short-term funding.

- Moderate policy - short-term funding is used to finance the fluctuating current assets and the permanent assets (current and non-current) are financed by long-term funding

21.2 The correct answer is:

- Increasing levels of long term borrowings.

CIMA define over-trading as "…where an entity enters into trading commitments in excess of its available short-term resources".

Even if an overtrading business operates at a profit, the lack of working capital may mean that they lack the cash to pay debts as they fall due - this can lead to apparently profitable businesses going into liquidation.

21.3 The correct answer is: 108 days.

This is calculated as:

46 days + 43 days − 67 days + 32 days + 54 days = 108 days.

21.4 The correct answer is: A dramatic reduction in sales revenue.

A company that overtrades is doing too much too quickly.

21.5 The correct answer is:

- Shareholders will not be happy as resources could be used elsewhere to generate a return.
- The entity has invested too much in receivables, inventory and cash and holds few payables.
- The entity has an excess of working capital.

21.6 The correct answer is: 115 days.

Inventory turnover period = 102 - 54 + 67 = 115 days

21.7 The correct answer is:

Inventory days   44.6
Trade receivables days   57.8

Inventory days = (inventory/ COS) × 365 days = (220/ 1,800) × 365 = 44.6 days

Trade receivable days = (average trade receivables/ credit sales for the year) × 365 days = (350/ 2,600 × 0.85) × 365 days = 57.8 days

21.8 The correct answer is:
- Inventory days plus accounts receivable days less accounts payable days.

21.9 The correct answer is:

Receivables days   24.9
Payables days   64.2

- Receivable days = (average trade receivables/credit sales for the year) * 365 days = (((800 + 840)/2)/12,000) * 365 days = 24.9 days

- Payable days = (average trade payables/purchases on credit for the year) * 365 days = (((1,120 + 1,160)/2)/(6,400 + 1,200 - 1,120)) * 365 = 64.2 days

Purchases on credit for the year are calculated by taking the 20X1 cost of sales and adding the 20X1 inventories and subtracting the 20X0 inventories.

21.10 The correct answer is:

- Sale of a non-current asset on credit at its carrying amount.

The receipt of the full amount of cash from a trade receivable will increase cash and reduce receivables by the same amount.

The payment of an account payable will reduce cash and reduce payables by the same amount.

The purchase of inventory on credit would increase inventory and increase payables by the same amount.

Hence all of these will have no impact on the amount of working capital.

22 Cash flow forecasts

22.1 The correct answer is:

- Expected gain on the disposal of a piece of land.

When preparing a cash forecast only CASH is considered. Here the question talks about a GAIN on disposal and gains are not cash. Gains are where the cash received is greater than the carrying amount of the asset.

22.2 The correct answer is: $5,500,000.

	$
Opening receivables cash received during year	460,000
Cash received ($5,400,000 × 20%)	1,080,000
11 months of credit sales ([$5,400,000 × 80%] × 11/12)	3,960,000
	5,500,000

22.3 The correct answer is: An expected gain on the disposal of an old factory site.

22.4 The correct answer is: Depreciation of the new rolling mill.

Depreciation is a non-cash item and should therefore be excluded from a cash flow forecast.

22.5 The correct answer is:

- Negotiate with the bank for a short-term loan to cover the deficit.

Since the cash flow problems appear to be temporary in nature, it is appropriate to use a short-term solution.

The acquistion of an asset under a finance lease, securing long term investment and a share issue are all long term sources of finance.

22.6 The correct answer is: $273,510.

Receivables at 31 March 20X7 = $290,510/ 365 days × 49 days = $39,000

Cash received is therefore:

	$
Opening receivables	22,000
Credit sales	290,510
Closing receivables	(39,000)
Cash received	273,510

22.7 The correct answer is: $'000: 395.

This is calculated as:

	$'000
Inventory b/f	39
Inventory purchased (balancing figure)	384
Inventory c/f	(51)
Inventory used	372
Payables b/f	58
Purchases (from inventory working)	384
Payables c/f	(47)
Cash paid	395

22.8 The correct answer is: $45,833.

Gross profit = 50% sales => Cost of sales = 50% sales.

Annual cost of sales = 50% × $1.1 million = $550,000

As inventories remain constant, this is also the annual purchase cost, which is spread evenly over the year.

Thus one month's purchases = $550,000/12 = $45,833

This is the value of one month's extra trade credit, i.e. the cash benefit to be derived from delaying payment by one month.

22.9 The correct answer is: $3,239.

Januray sales amount to: $12,500 and sales during February to December will be $3,409 per month ([$50,000 × 75%] / 11).

Therefore in March cash received will be 40% of February's sales plus 55% of March's sales = $3,239.

22.10 The correct answer is: $35,100.

April: Sales = $40,000; therefore cost of sales = $30,000 and closing payables = $4,500

May: Sales = $48,000; therefore cost of sales = $36,000 and closing payables = $5,400

PAYABLES ACCOUNT (MAY)

Cash (bal figure)	35,100	Opening balance	4,500
Closing	5,400	Cost of sales	36,000
	40,500		40,500

23 Cash management

23.1 The correct answer is:

- Compared with other types of loan it is quick and easy to set up.

Interest is only paid on the amount borrowed, not the full facility.

23.2 The correct answer is:

- Interest is payable on the total amount of the agreed overdraft limit rather than on the amount borrowed.

Interest is only payable on the amount borrowed rather than the agreed overdraft limit.

23.3 The correct answer is: Trade receivable factoring.

23.4 The correct answer is: Treasury bills.

23.5 The correct answer is:

The terms of an overdraft are more easily changed to accommodate different needs within the entity.

23.6 The correct answer is: Letter of credit.

This is also known as a documentary credit.

A bill of exchange is between a supplier and customer, is a written acknowledgement of debt (an IOU).

23.7 The correct answer is: Investment in equities.

Short-term cash surpluses will not normally be invested in equities owing to the risks associated with achieving a return over a short period.

23.8 The correct answer is: It is a method of providing medium-term export finance.

23.9 The correct answer is: Certificates of deposit are non-negotiable.

23.10 The correct answer is:

- A document issued by a bank on behalf of a customer authorising a person to draw money to a specified amount from its branches or correspondents, usually in another country, when the conditions set out in the document have been met.

Letters of credit provide a method of payment in international trade which gives the exporter a risk free method of obtaining credit.

24 Receivables and payables

24.1   The correct answer is: Deciding what credit limits customers should be given.

24.2   The correct answer is: Negotiation of the price of the goods.

The credit cycle begins with the receipt of the customer's order. Price negotiations take place prior to this point.

24.3   The correct answer is:

- Selling invoices to a finance company for less than their face value while continuing to collect the cash from the customer.

Here the entity maintains the administration of the sales ledger but sells selected invoices to the invoice discounter purely to obtain an advance of cash.

24.4   The correct answer is: The borrowing is repayable over a number of years.

Factoring is a short term method of raising finance.

24.5   The correct answers are:

- Difficulty in obtaining credit from new suppliers
- Reduction in credit rating

24.6   The correct answer is: $25,000.

(Total sales × 2%) + $5,000. 'Without recourse' means that the factor carries the risk of the irrecoverable debts.

24.7   The correct answer is: Saving of $46,000.

A saving of $36,000 ignores the effect of the changes on the level of inventories and payables.

Increases of $46,000 and $36,000 are wrong because they assume that the financing cost will increase not decrease.

Current level of receivables	$= \$2m \times \dfrac{90}{365}$	$= \$493,151$
New level of receivables	$= \$2m \times 80\% \times \dfrac{30}{365}$	$= \$131,507$
Current financing requirement	$= \$500,000 + \$493,150 - \$30,000$	$= \$963,150$
New financing requirement	$= \$400,000 + \$131,507 - \$24,000$	$= \$507,507$
Reduction in financing requirement	$= \$963,150 - \$507,507$	$= \$455,643$
Reduction in financing cost	$= \$455,643 \times 10\%$	$= \$45,564$ (round to $46,000).

24.8   The correct answer is: $28,800.

Factor advances 80% of $2,190,000 = $1,752,000

Trade receivables = 50/365 × $1,752,000 = $240,000
Interest at 12%   = $240,000 × 12%   = $28,800

24.9   The correct answer is: 78 days

$8,000 + purchases − $12,000 = COS = $103,628.

Balancing figure for credit purchases is 107,628.

Using the trade payable days formula: (23,000/107,628) × 365 days = 78 days.

24.10 The correct answers are:

- X Co will be dissatisfied with what NC owe them
- Overall NC are very good at paying suppliers within due dates

25 Managing inventory

25.1 The correct answer is:

- Loss of goodwill as a result of being unable to complete customer orders due to lack of inventory.

Insurance, storage and loss of interest are all costs of holding inventory. If inventory is held then customer orders will be complete and so no goodwill will be lost.

25.2 The correct answers are:

- Carriage inwards on raw materials delivered to factory
- Factory supervisors' salaries
- Factory heating and lighting
- Import duties on raw materials

Carriage outwards is charged to distribution and abnormal costs are not included in inventory.

25.3 The correct answer is: $8,500.

According to IAS 2, inventory should be valued at the lower of cost and net realisable value, so $8,500.

	$		$
Direct material ($3 * 1,000)	3,000	Selling price ($30 * 1,000)	30,000
Direct labour ($4 * 1,000)	4,000	Gross profit margin	*50%
		Wholesale price	15,000
Total direct costs	7,000	Trade discount	-30%
Factory overhead ($100,000 * 2%)	2,000	Net sales value	10,500
Total cost	9,000	Selling costs ($2 * 1,000)	-2,000
		Net realisable value	8,500

25.4 The correct answers are:

- Physical deterioration of inventory.
- Increases in the cost of raw materials.
- Errors in production or purchasing.

Physical deterioration of inventory would mean that goods might well not realise as much as it originally cost to buy or produce them.

Increases in cost may well mean than the margin of sales price over cost has been eroded away.

Errors in purchasing might mean that the goods will not realise the selling price originally budgeted. The most extreme case of this is goods becoming obsolete.

An increase in selling price of goods sold would increase net realisable value.

25.5 The correct answer is:

- The treatment is acceptable provided only production related overheads are included using a normal basis of activity to calculate the absorption rates.

Only production overheads can be included in value of inventory.

25.6 The correct answer is: 2,208 units.

$$EOQ = \sqrt{\frac{2C_oD}{C_h}}$$

$$= \sqrt{\frac{2 \times \$100 \times 39,000}{\$1.60}}$$

= 2,208 units

25.7 The correct answer is: 1,500 units.

The annual demand of 39,000 boxes is spread evenly over the year. Weekly demand is therefore 39,000/52 = 750 boxes per week.

It takes two weeks for an order to be delivered to JD's premises so JD needs to have 2 weeks × 750 = 1,500 boxes to make sure it never runs out of inventory.

25.8 The correct answer is: 866 units.

$$EOQ = \sqrt{\frac{2 \times \text{order cost} \times \text{demand}}{\text{holding cost}}}$$

$$EOQ = \sqrt{\frac{2 \times 150 \times 15,000}{\$6}}$$

EOQ = 866.

25.9 The correct answer is: $600.

Per IAS 2, inventories should be measured at the lower of cost and net realisable value.

	$
Cost	2.20
Net realisable value:	
Selling price	3.50
Less additional costs for repair and sale	(1.50)
	2.00

Therefore, inventories held at $2.00 each.
Total value 300 × $2.00 = $600.

25.10 The correct answer is: Plant lying idle will lead to a higher fixed overhead allocation to each unit.

26 Mixed Bank 1

26.1 The correct answer is: Priority given to different user groups in different countries.

26.2 The correct answers are:

- Information that is free from error.
- Information that is complete.

26.3 The correct answers are:

- Freehold buildings.
- Plant and machinery.

Buildings and plant and machinery have a finite useful life and are thus depreciated in accordance with IAS 16 *Property, plant and equipment.*

Freehold land has an indefinite life and is not depreciated.

Investment properties are not depreciated per IAS 40 *Investment property.*

26.4   The correct answer is: $225,000.

The assets need to be depreciated for the half year to 30 June 20X4 and the carrying amount compared to the fair value less costs to sell of $225,000 ($232,000 – $7,000).

The carrying amount at 30 June 20X4 is $235,000 ($250,000 – [$30,000 × 6/12]).

Therefore the assets should be valued at $225,000.

The value in use is irrelevant as the assets will be sold.

26.5   The correct answer is: Gain $60,000.

	$
Opening plan liabilities	5,500,000
Interest on b/d liabilities (4% × $5,500,000)	220,000
Current service cost	1,020,000
Benefits paid	(280,000)
Re-measurement gain (balancing figure)	(60,000)
Present value of liabilities at 31 December 20X2	6,400,000

26.6   The correct answer is: $39,600

	$
Consideration transferred	280,000
Non-controlling interest	64,800
Net assets	(306,000)
Goodwill	39,600

26.7   The correct answer is:

- Process of earmarking tax revenues for specific types of expenditure.

Hypothecation is also known as ring fencing and describes the situation where revenues raised from tax are used to finance specific types of expenditure. For example motorists in the city of London (in the United Kingdom) are charged a 'congestion charge' and revenues raised can only be spent on London transport.

26.8   The correct answer is:

- An individual purchases goods in a shop, the price includes VAT.

VAT is an indirect tax because it relates to consumption/ spending. VAT is collected by the shop and passed on to the tax authorities via its VAT return.

Corporate income tax, employee tax and capital gain tax are all direct taxes as they relate to income/ profits.

26.9   The correct answer is:

- Short-term financing of $1m; permanent financing of $14m.

Short-term finance is matched to fluctuating current assets.

A policy where short-term financing was $0.5m and permanent financing of $14.5m is a conservative policy.

Having short-term financing of $2m and permanent financing of $13m and short-term financing of $4m and permanent financing of $11m are both are aggressive policies.

26.10   The correct answer is: $7 decrease.

Cash flow if debts are factored:

90% of $90 received	$81
Current cash flow:	
40% of $100 paid in 30 days	$40
60% x 80% of $100 received later	$48
	$88

Difference = $7

27 Mixed Bank 2

27.1 The correct answer is: The International Accounting Standards Board.

The role of the IASB is to develop and publish International Financial Reporting Standards.

27.2 The correct answers are:

- Accruals
- Faithful representation
- Relevance

The underlying assumption is going concern.

27.3 The correct answer is:

- Shares in another company held as a short-term store of spare cash would most likely be classified as a current asset investment.

Freehold property, occupied by the entity, held for its investment potential is a tangible non-current asset.

Freehold property, not occupied by the entity, held for its investment potential is a tangible non-current asset that would, incidentally, appear to qualify as an investment property per IAS 40.

A limited edition delivery van used in the entity's operations is also a tangible non-current asset.

27.4 The correct answer is: Under current assets.

The assets of the retailing division should be removed from non-current assets and shown at their fair value under current assets, classified as 'non-current assets held for sale'.

27.5 The correct answer is: Gain $40,000.

	$'000
B/d plan assets	1,080
Benefits paid	(342)
Contributions paid	450
Interest income on plan assets	86
Re-measurement gain (balancing figure)	40
C/d plan assets	1,314

27.6 The correct answers are:

- Parent entity is itself partially owned but has consent from the non-controlling interest.
- Parent is itself a wholly owned subsidiary.

27.7 The correct answer is: Effective incidence.

Effective incidence describes the individual/ entity that bears the end cost of a tax whereas formal incidence describes the individual/ entity that has direct contact with the tax authorities.

27.8 The correct answer is: Sales tax.

Sales tax is an indirect tax because it relates to consumption/ spending. Withholding tax, employee tax and corporate income tax are all direct taxes as they relate to income/ profits.

27.9 The correct answer is: 114 days.

Inventory days	= $(8 \div (\$48m \times 60\%)) \times$ 365 days		= 101.4 days
Receivable days	= ($10/$48) $\times$ 365 days		= 76 days
Payable days	= $(5 \div (\$48 \times 60\%)) \times$ 365 days		= 63.4 days
Cash operating cycle	= 101.4 days	+ 76 days – 63.4 days	= 114 days

27.10 The correct answer is:

- The factoring company purchases a selection of invoices, at a discount, thus providing the client with a source of short-term finance.

BPP LEARNING MEDIA

True invoice discounting is a one-off arrangement made purely for the advance of cash to the client to cover a short-term cash shortfall.

While a factoring company may take over sales invoicing, this is an administrative service and has no financial component. It therefore has nothing to do with invoice discounting.

Enforcing correct administration is an administrative function that will be carried out by the factoring company if it is responsible for debt collection. It has nothing to do with the provision of finance.

Advancing finance to the client is effectively 'factor finance', or the provision of short-term finance against the total receivables ledger rather than against individual invoices.

28 Mixed Bank 3

28.1   The correct answer is: Rotation of lead audit partner every five years.

28.2   The correct answers are:

- Accounting standards will develop in a more coherent fashion.
- Different accounting presentation of transactions not currently covered by an IAS/IFRS should reduce.

The technical content of new standards, is becoming ever more demanding. Implementation problems will always remain. A conceptual framework can never make development easier or implementation more acceptable. It should, however, mean that standards are more coherent as a body of principles/ rules.

This coherence and common use of definitions and principles should also reduce confusing different presentations where no accounting standard currently exists.

28.3   The correct answer is: Property being constructed on behalf of third parties.

This would be accounted for under IAS 11 *Construction contracts* as a construction contract. This accounting standard is not examinable.. The other options are all forms of investment property.

28.4   The correct answer is: $45,000.

The assets of the manufacturing division should be valued at the lower of the carrying amount and the fair value less costs to sell.

For YS this is the lower of $443,000 and $398,000 ($423,000 – $25,000) and so an impairment loss of $45,000 should be recognised.

28.5   The correct answer is: $314,000.

	$'000
Current service cost	300,000
Interest on b/d liabilities (7% × $1,400,000)	98,000
Interest on b/d assets (7% × $1,200,000)	(84,000)
	314,000

28.6   The correct answer is: $25 million.

	CD $m	MB $m
Per question	26	12
Pre acquisition		(7)
		5
Group share of post acquisition reserves (60% × $5 million)	3	
Less impairment loss	(4)	
	25	

28.7   The correct answer is:

The amount of tax due to be paid and the amount actually collected.

Tax authorities always aim to minimise the tax gap.

28.8 The correct answer is: The end consumer.

Provided that the supplier of raw materials, the retailer and the wholesaler are registered for sales tax they merely act as tax collectors, it is the end consumer who suffers the tax.

28.9 The correct answer is: $6.750 million.

	$
Inventory ($30m × 0.7 × 2.5/12)	4.375m
Accounts receivable ($30m × 2/12)	5.000m
Accounts payable ($30m × 0.7 × 1.5/12)	(2.625m)
	6.750m

28.10 The correct answers are:

- Provision of finance against the client's outstanding receivables.
- Protection against irrecoverable debts.
- Administration of the client's invoicing and debt collection.

The factor is concerned with the receivables ledger department (not payables ledger) and can be involved in its administration.

Protection against irrecoverable debts is provided if factoring is "without recourse", and finance may be provided by making payments to the client before the debts are collected.

Credit rating information will normally be provided by a credit rating agency.

29 Mixed Bank 4

29.1 The correct answer is: Modified - qualified opinion (due to material misstatement).

The irrecoverable balance represents 20% of profit and therefore is material. As such a qualified opinion should be issued as the misstatement is material but not pervasive.

29.2 The correct answer is: Neutrality.

This ensures that the financial statements are free from bias and will therefore more closely reflect the activities of the entity throughout the period.

29.3 The correct answers are:

- Dr Deferred income, Cr Other income (if presented under a separate heading as income)
- Dr Deferred income, Cr The related expense (if presented as a deduction from the related expense)

Both methods are permitted under IAS 20 *Government Grants*.

29.4 Depreciation on assets classified as held for sale: $20,000 ($12,000 + $8,000)

Loss on adjustment in asset's value to fair value: $26,000

These are calculated as follows:

	$'000	$'000
Factory		
Cost	460	
Depreciation b/f	(23)	
Depreciation – year (460 × 2.5%)	(12)	
		425
Plant and equipment		
Cost	180	
Depreciation b/f	(140)	
Depreciation – year ([180 – 140] × 20%)	(8)	
		32
		457
Fair value of assets		431
Loss on adjustment in asset's value to fair value		(26)

29.5 The correct answers are:

- Current service cost
- Unwinding of discount on plan liabilities

Re-measurement of gain on plan liabilities is recognised in other comprehensive income.

Contributions paid into scheme increase plan assets and reduce entity's cash.

29.6 The correct answers are:

Cash and cash equivalents	$15,000	Debit
Consolidated trade receivables	$15,000	Credit

29.7 The correct answer is: A progressive tax.

A progressive tax structure exists where an increasing proportion of income is taken in tax as income rises. Here BM pays tax at a rate of 10% on taxable profits of $30,000 whilst BV pays tax at 12.5% on taxable profits of $60,000.

29.8 The correct answer is: Place of effective management.

In the event that an entity is resident in more than one country, the OECD Model Tax Convention states that the entity will be deemed to be resident only in the country of its effective management.

29.9 The correct answer is: $1,495,425.

$242,000 + $1,500,000 - ($1,500,000 \times 60/365) = $1,495,425

29.10 The correct answer is: 44.9%.

Payment will be made 30 days early.

Number of compounding periods $= \dfrac{365}{30} = 12.167$

$$1 + r = \left(\dfrac{1.00}{0.97}\right)^{12.167}$$
$$= 1.4486$$
$$\therefore r = 44.86\%$$

30 Mixed Bank 5

30.1 The correct answer is: ISA 700 *Forming an opinion and reporting on financial statements* prescribes its use.

The ISA imposes a requirement to report on the truth and fairness (present fairly) of the financial statements. This is not defined by legislation.

30.2 The correct answer is: Loss on closure of bottling division.

This must be disclosed on the face of the statement of profit or loss per IFRS 5.

IAS 1 requires disclosure of items which are of such size, nature or importance that disclosure is necessary to explain performance of entity. However, such disclosure may be in the notes, and does not have to be on the face of the statement of profit or loss.

30.3 The correct answer is: $4.95 million.

Capitalisation rate = (100/180 × 10%) + (80/180 × 8%) = 9%

	$m
$40m × 9%	3.6
$30m × 9% x 6/12	1.35
	4.95

30.4 The correct answers are:

- Long-term bank deposits.
- Amounts payable to a foreign leasing company.
- The balance due from an overseas company in relation to export sales.

An acquisition of a new machine from a foreign supplier is a non-monetary item.

30.5 The correct answer is: $204,000.

Non-current asset costs

	$		$
Opening balance	1,096,000	Disposal	150,000
Revaluation (240 - 140)	100,000		
Cash paid (bal fig)	204,000	Closing balance	1,250,000
	1,400,000		1,400,000

30.6 The correct answer is: $1,624,000.

	OP	ST
	$000	$000
At year end	1,360	920
PPE adjustment (W1)		(60)
Pre-acquisition retained earnings		(560)
		360
Group share of post-acquisition retained earnings (90% × $360,000)	324	
Consolidated retained earnings	1,624	

W1	$000
Unrealised profit on PPE transfer $200 - $120 =	80
Less proportion depreciated 80/4	(20)
	60

30.7 The correct answer is: $22,250.

This is calculated as follows:

	$
Accounting profit	72,000
Add: disallowable expenditure:	
Entertaining	15,000
Accounting depreciation	12,000
	99,000
Less: tax depreciation (40,000 × 25%)	(10,000)
	89,000
Tax (25% × $89,000)	22,250

30.8 The correct answer is: $16,000.

	$
Output tax (400,000 / 2) × 15% =	30,000
Input tax 28,000 / 2	(14,000)
	16,000

30.9 The correct answers are:

reducing receivables.
reducing inventory.
increasing the credit period from the company's trade suppliers.

If the credit period from trade suppliers increases, it provides a source of finance for the company.

If the inventory levels reduce, less working capital is blocked in inventory.

If the receivables reduce, they pay early/on time and this improves cashflow.

30.10 The correct answers are:

- Average cost calculates a new weighted average cost calculated upon each delivery.
- FIFO assumes that inventory is used in the order in which it is delivered.

Replacement cost is valuing inventory at the current cost of acquisition - i.e. how much would it cost to replace the inventory you have today.

Inventory may be valued using standard cost provided that the standard cost is kept up to date.

The net realisable value is calculated on selling price less costs of completion of the inventory items which are yet to be incurred, less any selling costs. NRV should be used if this figure is less than the cost of inventory, therefore this is also incorrect.

31 Mixed Bank 6

31.1   The correct answer is: None of the above statements are correct.

The audit report lends credibility to financial statements, but it does not give 100% assurance that all errors or irregularities have been identified or they were adjusted if discovered. It is not necessary that the company has followed the provisions of IFRSs as the auditor may have concurred that a departure from the standards was necessary in order that a true and fair view was given.

31.2   The correct answer is: An upward revaluation of the company's assets.

It is the only one of the four options that is a gain or loss accounted for as 'other comprehensive income'.

31.3   The correct answer is: Internally developed brands must not be capitalised.

Negative goodwill must firstly be re-assessed to ensure that it has not resulted due to an error and should then be credited to profit or loss in the period in which it arose.

Purchased goodwill must be capitalised as an intangible non-current asset and reviewed annually for impairment.

Internally generated goodwill cannot be recognised in the financial statement and may definitely not be revalued.

31.4   The correct answer is: $27,500.

This is calculated as the charge for the year of $25,000 plus the under provision in respect of the prior year ($7,500 - $5,000).

31.5   The correct answer is: Profit on sale of a motor vehicle.

The profit on sale of the motor vehicle is a non-cash item which has invreased profit before tax. It should be deducted from the profit before tax figure when arriving at net cash flow from operating activities.

The surplus on the revaluation of property is also a non-cash item. This does not however impact the profit before tax and so is excluded from the statement of cash flows.

31.6   The correct answer is: $25,900.

	$000
Cost of investment	25,000
Share of post-acquisition reserves 30% × ($6,500 – $3,500)	900
	25,900

31.7   The correct answer is: Capital gains tax.

Direct taxes relate to taxes charged on income or profits, such as capital gains tax. Value added tax, excise duties and property tax all relate to taxes on spending and are examples of an indirect tax.

31.8 The correct answer is: UK.

As the company's place of management - its head office - is in London, it will be considered to be UK resident. If the company wanted to establish residence in Switzerland, it would have to move its head office functions to Switzerland.

31.9 The correct answer is: Advances against collections.

The question asked which of the methods would NOT reduce the risks of irrecoverable debts when trading overseas. Export factoring, forfaiting and documentary credits are all methods of insuring against irrecoverable debts risk from overseas receivables.

Advance against collections from a factor or a discount house can reduce the amount of funds an entity has invested in foreign receivables, but it does not reduce the risk of irrecoverable debts.

31.10 The correct answer is: The cost of holding one unit of inventory for one year.

d is the Annual Demand.

c is the Cost of Ordering.

$$EOQ = \sqrt{\frac{2CoD}{Ch}}$$

32 Mixed Bank 7

32.1 The correct answer is: Financial interest in a client's affairs.

Preparing accounts for an audit client is a self-review threat.

Becoming too friendly with client staff is a familiarity threat.

Being threatened with litigation is an intimidation threat.

32.2 The correct answer is: $92,000 gain.

The write down would be treated as an expense in profit or loss; the upwards revaluation is recorded as other comprehensive income.

32.3 The correct answers are:

- The benefits flowing from the completed development are expected to be less than its cost
- Funds are unlikely to be available to complete the development

A project that is not commercially viable would not be capitalised.

The company must have adequate resources to fund the project for it to be capitalised.

32.4 The correct answer is:

- Lightning struck one of HL's production facilities on 31 January 20X9 and caused a serious fire. The fire destroyed half of the factory and its machinery. Output was severely reduced for six months.

An adjusting event is an event that provides further evidence of a condition that already existed at the reporting date.

A non-adjusting event relates to the situation where the condition did not exist at the reporting date.

32.5 The correct answers are:

- Bank current account in domestic currency.
- Bank overdraft.
- Petty cash float.

Bank current account in foreign currency.

The short term deposit is not included in cash. It could potentially have been included as a cash equivalent however for this to be the case it would need to be repayable on demand. This is only the case if it can be withdrawn without notice (in practice within 24 hours) but the deposit in question has a three month notice period.

Therefore it is neither cash nor a cash equivalent.

32.6 The correct answer is: $87,500

	$
Cost of investment	70,000
Share of post-acquisition reserves 35% × (130-80)	17,500
	87,500

32.7 The correct answer is:

- Payment of tax on a capital gain can be delayed if the full proceeds from the sale of an asset are reinvested in a replacement asset.

32.8 The correct answer is: Sets out which tax authority has jurisdiction.

A double taxation treaty existing between two countries will establish in which country a company trading in both areas will be primarily taxed.

This may mean that withholding tax is reduced or not charged. Under the treaty a company which does business abroad may pay foreign taxes but will get relief for them.

32.9 The correct answer is: Credit insurance

Credit insurance is an insurance which can be taken out (at a cost to the entity) which the entity can claim on in the event that an overseas receivable fails to pay the amounts owed.

Credit insurance is therefore not a source of finance.

32.10 The correct answer is: 8,000 units.

The cost of holding one item in inventory for a year is $4. Note that this is also subject to the discounts.

The EOQ without the discounts is 800, but this is not the most economic order quantity when the discounts are taken into account.

Quantity	800	1,000	4,000	8,000
No. of orders	25	20	5	3
Order	$1,600	$1,280	$320	$192
Holding*	$1,600	$1,980	$7,840	$15,520
Purchase	$800,000	$792,000	$784,000	$776,000
Cost	$803,200	$795,260	$792,160	$791,712

*Remember that holding cost = (Order quantity × Cost of holding one unit for a year) / 2 and don't forget to take account of the discount as well.

Therefore 8,000 units give the lowest cost.

If the company places orders of 8,000 units, 3 orders will need to be made to meet the 20,000 unit requirement.

33 Mixed Bank 8

33.1 The correct answer is: Reliability.

The fifth fundamental principle is professional behaviour.

33.2 The correct answers are:

- It can explain factors which have contributed to company results.
- Users can assess the future risks and rewards associated with the business.

By splitting out the company's results by region and product a more in-depth understanding of the make-up of the results is obtained. Segment reporting helps users of the financial statements to assess which regions and products will improve or have a negative impact on the company's future performance.

33.3   The correct answer is: $10 million.

The impairment loss is applied first against the goodwill and then against the other non-current assets on a pro-rata basis. It will be allocated as follows:

	$
Building	10
Plant and equipment	5
Goodwill	5
	20

The carrying amount of the building will then become $10 million (20 – 10).

33.4   The correct answers are:

- Opening new trading operations
- Announcement of plan to discontinue an operation
- Expropriation (seizure) of major assets by government

An adjusting event is an event that provides further evidence of a condition that already existed at the reporting date.

A non-adjusting event relates to the situation where the condition did not exist at the reporting date.

33.5   The correct answer is: $180,000.

Non current assets – cost

	$		$
B/d	180,000	Disposals	80,000
Therefore purchases	140,000	C/d	240,000
	320,000		320,000

Depreciation

	$		$
		B/d	120,000
Disposals	50,000	Charge for the year	70,000
c/d	140,000		
	190,000		190,000

Disposals

	$		$
Cost	80,000	Accumulated depreciation	50,000
		Proceeds	20,000
		Therefore loss	10,000
	80,000		80,000

	$
Cash from operations	300,000
Cash inflow:	
Disposal proceeds	20,000
	320,000
Cash outflow:	
purchases of non-current assets	-140,000
Therefore net cash increase	180,000

Note that adjustments for depreciation and loss on disposal will already be included in final figure for net cash flow from operating activities.

33.6 The correct answer is: $141,000.

	$'000
Consideration transferred	120
Share of post-acquisition retained earnings 40% × (140 - 60)	24
Unrealised profit 30 × 25% × 40%	(3)
Investment in associate	141

33.7 The correct answer is: $10,000.

Tax payable by shareholders:

	$
Dividend received	150,000
Tax credit (150,000 / 75 * 25)	50,000
Gross dividend	200,000
Tax at 30%	60,000
Less tax credit	(50,000)
Tax to pay	10,000

33.8 The correct answer is: $30,000.

Tax due in Country Y:

	$
Gross dividend	100,000
Add: underlying tax	20,000
	120,000
Tax at 40%	48,000
Less: DTR for WHT	(10,000)
Less: DTR for ULT	(20,000)
Tax payable	18,000

Double tax relief = 10,000 + 20,000 = $30,000

33.9 The correct answer is: Both statements are true.

It is important not to confuse the coupon rate and the yield to maturity especially when calculating the selling price of a bond.

33.10 The correct answer is: (i) only, the order quantity.

The EOQ model finds order quantity only.

The reorder levels are normally set by reference to lead time and demand in lead time, buffer inventory is decided by management.

Mathematical tables

PRESENT VALUE TABLE

Present value of 1.00 unit of currency, that is $(1+r)^{-n}$ where r = interest rate; n = number of periods until payment or receipt.

Periods	Interest rates (r)									
(n)	1%	2%	3%	4%	5%	6%	7%	8%	9%	10%
1	0.990	0.980	0.971	0.962	0.952	0.943	0.935	0.926	0.917	0.909
2	0.980	0.961	0.943	0.925	0.907	0.890	0.873	0.857	0.842	0.826
3	0.971	0.942	0.915	0.889	0.864	0.840	0.816	0.794	0.772	0.751
4	0.961	0.924	0.888	0.855	0.823	0.792	0.763	0.735	0.708	0.683
5	0.951	0.906	0.863	0.822	0.784	0.747	0.713	0.681	0.650	0.621
6	0.942	0.888	0.837	0.790	0.746	0.705	0.666	0.630	0.596	0.564
7	0.933	0.871	0.813	0.760	0.711	0.665	0.623	0.583	0.547	0.513
8	0.923	0.853	0.789	0.731	0.677	0.627	0.582	0.540	0.502	0.467
9	0.914	0.837	0.766	0.703	0.645	0.592	0.544	0.500	0.460	0.424
10	0.905	0.820	0.744	0.676	0.614	0.558	0.508	0.463	0.422	0.386
11	0.896	0.804	0.722	0.650	0.585	0.527	0.475	0.429	0.388	0.350
12	0.887	0.788	0.701	0.625	0.557	0.497	0.444	0.397	0.356	0.319
13	0.879	0.773	0.681	0.601	0.530	0.469	0.415	0.368	0.326	0.290
14	0.870	0.758	0.661	0.577	0.505	0.442	0.388	0.340	0.299	0.263
15	0.861	0.743	0.642	0.555	0.481	0.417	0.362	0.315	0.275	0.239
16	0.853	0.728	0.623	0.534	0.458	0.394	0.339	0.292	0.252	0.218
17	0.844	0.714	0.605	0.513	0.436	0.371	0.317	0.270	0.231	0.198
18	0.836	0.700	0.587	0.494	0.416	0.350	0.296	0.250	0.212	0.180
19	0.828	0.686	0.570	0.475	0.396	0.331	0.277	0.232	0.194	0.164
20	0.820	0.673	0.554	0.456	0.377	0.312	0.258	0.215	0.178	0.149

Periods	Interest rates (r)									
(n)	11%	12%	13%	14%	15%	16%	17%	18%	19%	20%
1	0.901	0.893	0.885	0.877	0.870	0.862	0.855	0.847	0.840	0.833
2	0.812	0.797	0.783	0.769	0.756	0.743	0.731	0.718	0.706	0.694
3	0.731	0.712	0.693	0.675	0.658	0.641	0.624	0.609	0.593	0.579
4	0.659	0.636	0.613	0.592	0.572	0.552	0.534	0.516	0.499	0.482
5	0.593	0.567	0.543	0.519	0.497	0.476	0.456	0.437	0.419	0.402
6	0.535	0.507	0.480	0.456	0.432	0.410	0.390	0.370	0.352	0.335
7	0.482	0.452	0.425	0.400	0.376	0.354	0.333	0.314	0.296	0.279
8	0.434	0.404	0.376	0.351	0.327	0.305	0.285	0.266	0.249	0.233
9	0.391	0.361	0.333	0.308	0.284	0.263	0.243	0.225	0.209	0.194
10	0.352	0.322	0.295	0.270	0.247	0.227	0.208	0.191	0.176	0.162
11	0.317	0.287	0.261	0.237	0.215	0.195	0.178	0.162	0.148	0.135
12	0.286	0.257	0.231	0.208	0.187	0.168	0.152	0.137	0.124	0.112
13	0.258	0.229	0.204	0.182	0.163	0.145	0.130	0.116	0.104	0.093
14	0.232	0.205	0.181	0.160	0.141	0.125	0.111	0.099	0.088	0.078
15	0.209	0.183	0.160	0.140	0.123	0.108	0.095	0.084	0.079	0.065
16	0.188	0.163	0.141	0.123	0.107	0.093	0.081	0.071	0.062	0.054
17	0.170	0.146	0.125	0.108	0.093	0.080	0.069	0.060	0.052	0.045
18	0.153	0.130	0.111	0.095	0.081	0.069	0.059	0.051	0.044	0.038
19	0.138	0.116	0.098	0.083	0.070	0.060	0.051	0.043	0.037	0.031
20	0.124	0.104	0.087	0.073	0.061	0.051	0.043	0.037	0.031	0.026

Cumulative present value of 1.00 unit of currency per annum, Receivable or Payable at the end of each year for n years $\frac{1-(1+r)^{-n}}{r}$

Periods (n)	Interest rates (r)									
	1%	2%	3%	4%	5%	6%	7%	8%	9%	10%
1	0.990	0.980	0.971	0.962	0.952	0.943	0.935	0.926	0.917	0.909
2	1.970	1.942	1.913	1.886	1.859	1.833	1.808	1.783	1.759	1.736
3	2.941	2.884	2.829	2.775	2.723	2.673	2.624	2.577	2.531	2.487
4	3.902	3.808	3.717	3.630	3.546	3.465	3.387	3.312	3.240	3.170
5	4.853	4.713	4.580	4.452	4.329	4.212	4.100	3.993	3.890	3.791
6	5.795	5.601	5.417	5.242	5.076	4.917	4.767	4.623	4.486	4.355
7	6.728	6.472	6.230	6.002	5.786	5.582	5.389	5.206	5.033	4.868
8	7.652	7.325	7.020	6.733	6.463	6.210	5.971	5.747	5.535	5.335
9	8.566	8.162	7.786	7.435	7.108	6.802	6.515	6.247	5.995	5.759
10	9.471	8.983	8.530	8.111	7.722	7.360	7.024	6.710	6.418	6.145
11	10.368	9.787	9.253	8.760	8.306	7.887	7.499	7.139	6.805	6.495
12	11.255	10.575	9.954	9.385	8.863	8.384	7.943	7.536	7.161	6.814
13	12.134	11.348	10.635	9.986	9.394	8.853	8.358	7.904	7.487	7.103
14	13.004	12.106	11.296	10.563	9.899	9.295	8.745	8.244	7.786	7.367
15	13.865	12.849	11.938	11.118	10.380	9.712	9.108	8.559	8.061	7.606
16	14.718	13.578	12.561	11.652	10.838	10.106	9.447	8.851	8.313	7.824
17	15.562	14.292	13.166	12.166	11.274	10.477	9.763	9.122	8.544	8.022
18	16.398	14.992	13.754	12.659	11.690	10.828	10.059	9.372	8.756	8.201
19	17.226	15.679	14.324	13.134	12.085	11.158	10.336	9.604	8.950	8.365
20	18.046	16.351	14.878	13.590	12.462	11.470	10.594	9.818	9.129	8.514

Periods (n)	Interest rates (r)									
	11%	12%	13%	14%	15%	16%	17%	18%	19%	20%
1	0.901	0.893	0.885	0.877	0.870	0.862	0.855	0.847	0.840	0.833
2	1.713	1.690	1.668	1.647	1.626	1.605	1.585	1.566	1.547	1.528
3	2.444	2.402	2.361	2.322	2.283	2.246	2.210	2.174	2.140	2.106
4	3.102	3.037	2.974	2.914	2.855	2.798	2.743	2.690	2.639	2.589
5	3.696	3.605	3.517	3.433	3.352	3.274	3.199	3.127	3.058	2.991
6	4.231	4.111	3.998	3.889	3.784	3.685	3.589	3.498	3.410	3.326
7	4.712	4.564	4.423	4.288	4.160	4.039	3.922	3.812	3.706	3.605
8	5.146	4.968	4.799	4.639	4.487	4.344	4.207	4.078	3.954	3.837
9	5.537	5.328	5.132	4.946	4.772	4.607	4.451	4.303	4.163	4.031
10	5.889	5.650	5.426	5.216	5.019	4.833	4.659	4.494	4.339	4.192
11	6.207	5.938	5.687	5.453	5.234	5.029	4.836	4.656	4.486	4.327
12	6.492	6.194	5.918	5.660	5.421	5.197	4.988	4.793	4.611	4.439
13	6.750	6.424	6.122	5.842	5.583	5.342	5.118	4.910	4.715	4.533
14	6.982	6.628	6.302	6.002	5.724	5.468	5.229	5.008	4.802	4.611
15	7.191	6.811	6.462	6.142	5.847	5.575	5.324	5.092	4.876	4.675
16	7.379	6.974	6.604	6.265	5.954	5.668	5.405	5.162	4.938	4.730
17	7.549	7.120	6.729	6.373	6.047	5.749	5.475	5.222	4.990	4.775
18	7.702	7.250	6.840	6.467	6.128	5.818	5.534	5.273	5.033	4.812
19	7.839	7.366	6.938	6.550	6.198	5.877	5.584	5.316	5.070	4.843
20	7.963	7.469	7.025	6.623	6.259	5.929	5.628	5.353	5.101	4.870